HITLER:
STALIN'S STOOGE

HITLER:
STALIN'S STOOGE

HOW STALIN PLANNED TO USE
HITLER TO CONQUER EUROPE

James B. Edwards

cp
Aventine Press

Published by Aventine Press
1023 4th Ave. #204
San Diego, CA 92101, USA

www.aventinepress.com

ISBN: 1-59330-144-8
Printed in the United States of America

ACKNOWLEDGMENTS

I want to thank the following people for helping me put the book together. The Gulag charts and tables were originally developed by Rollin W. Gillespie; one of the world's leading pioneer space scientists. Among his many accomplishments were the early design of a comprehensive space transportation system and the development of the basic trajectory equations used in interplanetary flight. When Kennedy was setting up NASA, he told his staff to: "Go out and round up all the Rollin Gillespie's!"

Lewey Gilstrap prepared the spreadsheet program used to calculate the numbers of arrests, deaths and releases from the prison camps. Lewey Gilstrap was one of the pioneers in the field of artificial intelligence. He co-founded Adaptronics, Inc., who applied artificial neural networks and other artificial intelligence techniques to problems in aerospace, manufacturing, medical diagnostics, and defense. He is a member of the Johns Hopkins University Practitioner Faculty in Information Technology, teaching courses in artificial intelligence and information technology to masters degree students in Business Administration and Information Technology.

Dr. Albert L. Weeks, professor emeritus, New York University, has studied Soviet Russia for more than fifty years and is an expert in the field. He is the author of many books including the recent *Stalin's Other War* and *Russia's Lifeline: Lend-Lease Aid to the U.S.S.R. in World War II.*

David Fletcher, The Tank Museum, Bennington, Dorset, UK.

Frontispiece
Massed BT-7s parade through Moscow's Red Square on May
Day 1940 (top) and May Day 1941 (bottom). Courtesy: The Tank
Museum, Bovington, Dorset, U.K.

CONTENTS

TABLES AND FIGURES

INTRODUCTION

Hitler was the stooge Stalin used to start World War II. World War II was to be Stalin's instrument of conquest. Stalin planned a World War I redux that would leave an exhausted and helpless Europe ripe for Communist takeover. The Treaty of Versailles had forbidden Germany to have a strong army or any offensive weapons, such as military aircraft, tanks, heavy artillery, and submarines. Versailles had created starvation as well as economic, social, and political chaos in Germany and filled the people with a terrible thirst for revenge. Stalin saw a vengeful Germany as the perfect catalyst to trigger a new war. In great secrecy during the 1920s, Stalin gave the future Wehrmacht and Luftwaffe all the facilities and equipment they needed in the Soviet Union to rebuild their military machine. Stalin saw Hitler and the Nazis's vengeance crusade as the perfect instrument to achieve his ends.

In the 1920s and 1930s, Stalin pursued a long-range plan of conquest:

1. To build the most powerful political party and control apparatus in the world – the Communist Party of the Soviet Union (CPSU) and the political police – the NKVD.
2. To build the most powerful industrial machine in the world – a giant arsenal.
3. To build the most powerful military machine in the world – the Red Army and the Red Air Force.

4. To bring Hitler and the Nazis to power and use them to start World War II.
5. To crush an exhausted Europe, at the opportune moment in the war, with the mighty Red Army and Red Air Force.
6. To occupy and control Europe with the CPSU/NKVD apparatus.

In the 1930s, Stalin created the mightiest military machine in the world. Giant tank and aircraft factories were built all over the Soviet Union. Millions were inducted in the Red Army; tens of millions were trained in the para-military Osoaviakhim. Millions were recruited into the NKVD. During the Great Terror (1934-1938) millions of people were executed or shipped off to the slave labor camps in the vast Siberian Gulag. Stalin murdered tens of millions of people putting this giant apparatus into operation. In 1941, this gigantic machine was poised waiting to seize Europe.

The first section of the book describes:
1. Lenin's and Stalin's attempts to capture Germany in the 1920s.
2. Stalin's consolidation of power in the Great Purges of the 1930s.
3. Stalin's role in maneuvering Hitler into starting World War II.
4. Stalin' s strategies to seize Europe at the optimum point in the war,
5. Russian and German military equipment and tactics.

If as he planned, Stalin had attacked before Hitler did in 1940 or 1941, he would have almost certainly beaten Germany and conquered Western Europe. What Stalin did to the Russian people in the 1930s, he would have done to the Europeans in the 1940s. He would have imposed on Europe another "Great Terror" such as the one he had just imposed on his own people. Since the Europeans, unlike the Russians, were not accustomed to centuries of control and repression, the terror would have been, by necessity, far more severe.

The second section of the book tries to show what would have happened to the people of Europe in the 1940s and beyond had Stalin been able to impose his monstrous system on them. It tries to explain the fundamental nature of the system Lenin and Stalin created and to describe the incredible slaughter and suffering it caused. Attention is focused on the vast Gulag and the tens of millions of innocent people who perished in this frozen hell.

At Solovki, one of the earliest Gulag camps, there was a huge sign that captured the essence of the Communist system: **"WITH AN IRON FIST, WE WILL LEAD HUMANITY TO HAPPINESS"**

Nobody knows how many people the CPSU murdered between 1917 and 1991. As you will see in the charts and tables, our calculations (originally done in 1970) indicated that the Bolshevik regime killed approximately 130,000,000 people between 1917 and 1991. Our calculations were recently confirmed by one of the world's leading authorities on the Bolshevik slaughter, Roman Krutsyk, Chairman of Kiev Memorial, who said: "You're absolutely right – the figure is about 130 000 000." (E-mail: "UCCA"ucca@i.kiev.ua dated 4 April 2005) Mr. Krutsyk estimates that "50 million ethnic Ukrainians within the borders of the Soviet Union" were killed by the Bolsheviks in this 1917-1991 period.

To lend perspective to these numbers, consider the fact that the total casualties in World War I and World War II were 65,000,000 (WW I:15,000,000; WW II: 50,000,000.)

Utopia Empowered became Murder Incorporated!

During Collectivization, people were being executed, starved, or shipped to the Gulag by the millions. When the starving people started eating dogs and cats, the Party killed all the dogs and cats. When the people started eating birds, the Party killed all the birds. When the people started eating orphan children, the Party shot or poisoned all the orphan children.

During the Purges, about ten percent of the population of the Soviet Union (approximately 15,000,000) were executed outright, or shipped off to the Gulag to be worked to death. After World War II, the Gulag population probably reached approximately 40 million people.

In the Gulag, guards and criminals killed prisoners for diversion. Notorious Magadan commandant Ivan Nikishov, entertained himself by dancing around the prisoner formations, raining obscenities on them and shooting them at random. In 1944, Vice-President Henry Wallace and Professor Owen Lattimore visited Magadan; Nikishov was their host. Wallace found Magadan idyllic, noting approvingly how Nikishov "gamboled about, enjoying the wonderful air." Lattimore admired Nikishov's "trained and sensitive interest in art and music and a deep sense of civic responsibility." Nikishov had set up a "Potemkin" camp; all the prisoners and guards were NKVD; his guests were completely duped.
Robert Conquest, *The Great Terror,* pp. 353,354.

Some post-World War II history of the CPSU and the KGB are covered; but primary attention is focused on the activities of the CPSU and the NKVD during the 1930s. Though there were bureaucratic reorganizations and name changes, nothing fundamental about the CPSU or the NKVD/KGB changed until their demise.

What I've tried to do is come up with some new perspectives on old material, in hopes that better researchers than I will pursue the truth. Most of the basic information has been available since the 1930s and 1940s. The liberal establishment have been unwilling to face the ugly truths about the great utopian experiment they so admire.

At best, they are like Jean-Paul Sartre, who said that even if the stories of the Gulag were true, French workers should not be told – they might become anti-Soviet.

At worst, they are like Communist playwright Bertolt Brecht. When Brecht was told that Stalin had sent thousands of innocents to the Gulag, he replied: "The more innocent they are, the more they deserve to die."

Though numerous sources were used in developing the manuscript, most of the fundamental data can be confirmed by reading the following books, cited in the bibliography:

Robert Conquest, *The Great Terror*

R. J. Rummell, *Lethal Politics.*

Aleksandr I. Solzhenitsyn, *The Gulag Archipelago, 1918-1956, The Gulag Archipelago Two.*

Viktor Suvorov, *Icebreaker, Who Started the Second World War?*

Ernst Topitsch, *Stalin's War.*

Albert L. Weeks, *Stalin's Other War."*

"EMINENCE GRIS"

"If there is one place where a start can be made to arouse Europe to revolution, that place is Germany---and victory of the revolution in Germany will guarantee the victory of world revolution."
Stalin, *Sochineniya*, Vol.6, p.267.

Stalin brought Hitler to power and maneuvered him into starting World War II. All studies of Communism have shown that the long-range objective of the Communist Party of the Soviet Union (CPSU) was world conquest. Lenin made this clear in a speech delivered in 1920:

"[In November 1917] we knew that our victory will be a lasting victory only when our undertaking will conquer the whole world, because we have launched it exclusively counting on world revolution."
Lenin, *Polnoe sobraniesochinenii*, vol. 42, 1.

Lenin believed that a World War I devastated Europe was ripe for Communist conquest. Lenin and Stalin always believed Germany was the key to seizing control of Europe. Throughout 1918-1919, Lenin tried to overthrow the tottering German Republic by staging a Bolshevik coup as he had in Russia in 1917. All over Germany there were pitched battles between the troops of the Communist's Spartakists and the Republic's Freikorps. The Freikorps was made up largely of veteran "stosstruppen" – specially trained shocktroops who had spearheaded the German 1918 Spring offensive. They trounced the Spartakists; temporarily foiling Lenin's plans.

However, chaos continued to reign in Germany. Watching the growing Bolshevik strength, Poland feared the rebirth of a strong imperialist Russia that would be a threat to their newly acquired independence. In the Spring of 1920, the Poles allied themselves with the Ukrainian nationalist forces who had revolted against the Bolsheviks and were attempting to break away from Russia and create an independent Ukrainian Republic. Lenin sent the Red Army under the command of Stalin and General Tukhachevsky to put down the Ukrainian revolt and chase out the Poles. The revolt was crushed and the Polish Army retreated toward home with the Red Army in hot pursuit. Lenin saw this as another opportunity to seize control of Germany. Germany was still in political, economic, and social turmoil, and in Lenin's eyes a prime target for revolutionary takeover. He planned to march the Red Army through Poland, link up with still powerful Bolshevik forces in Germany and seize control directly.

The Poles, however, took umbrage to being used as an access highway to Germany. In a huge battle outside Warsaw, the Polish Army trounced the Red Army, and sent it reeling back to Russia. It was a devastating blow to Stalin's reputation, and aroused in him an enduring hatred of the Poles, for which they were to later pay a terrible price at places like the Katyn Forest. The Polish debacle convinced Lenin that the most feasible way to seize Germany and Europe would be to bring about another great European war. He figured it would be a rerun of World War I in which the Europeans would eventually bleed each other to death and be helpless to a Bolshevik takeover. This became the Bolshevik master plan, which Stalin relentlessly pursued throughout the 1920s and 1930s.

Due to the still fresh memories of the horrors of World War I, during the 1920s and 1930s democratic socialism, pacifism, disarmament, and peace at almost any price were the prevailing sentiments in Europe. Stalin considered European social democrats and pacifists the greatest obstacle to a new European war. In November 1927 he stated:

"It is impossible to finish with capitalism without first finishing with social democratism in the workers' movement." (Pravda, No. 255, 6/7 Nov. 1927.) Again, in 1928, Stalin reiterated: "---first of all, the struggle with social democratization along all lines, including and following from this exposure of bourgeois pacifism." Stalin, *Sochineniya,* Vol.II, p.202.

Marx and Engels had predicted a world war that would last "fifteen, twenty, fifty years," leading to "general exhaustion and creation of conditions for the final victory of the working class." Karl Marks and Friedrich Engels, *WORKS,* Ch. 21, p.351.

In the 1920s, Stalin decided to support Hitler and the Nazis rise to power as the best means to start the war he thought would destroy the entire European political and social structure. The Nazi Party and the German Communist Party hated the Social Democrat Party and often cooperated in hamstringing its programs. In November 1932, they worked together to organize a crippling transport strike in Berlin. In the German parliamentary elections of 1932-1933, Stalin ordered the German Communist Party to actively cooperate with the Nazis against the Social Democrats.(Alan Bullock, *HITLER,* pp. 210, 230.) The Social Democrats were for peace; the Nazis were hell-bent on avenging "the shame of Versailles." After Hitler became Kanzler, the new Party line portrayed him as the "icebreaker of the revolution." Hitler would start the great war that would lead to the revolution. It was fundamental Marxism-Leninism.

As Leon Trotsky said: "Without Stalin there would have been no Hitler, there would have been no Gestapo!" (Bulletin of the Opposition [BO], Nos.52-53, Oct, 1936.) During the 1920s, Hitler and the National Socialists Workers Party, the Nazis, grew in strength as they battled the Communists for control of Germany. In the 1920s and 1930s, they came to view the Communists as their principal long-range enemies and rivals for control of Europe. Thus, in the 1920s, Hitler's crusade became twofold: (a) to avenge the shameful Treaty of Versailles that had all but destroyed Germany after World War I; (b) to destroy Communism, and to occupy and exploit the great agricultural and industrial resources of the Soviet Union west of the Urals. Stalin saw Hitler's goals as the perfect vehicle to achieve his own goals. So, during the 1920s and 1930s, Stalin helped Germany rebuild and train the new Wehrmacht, Luftwaffe, and Kriegsmarine; the NKVD trained the Gestapo; Germany was supplied with any needed raw materials. Stalin became the "eminence gris" behind Hitler's rise to power.

To seize and control Europe, the Soviet Union would have to have the most powerful industrial, military, and political apparatus in the world. To achieve this, Stalin set out to build a massive industrial base, to industrialize agriculture, to create the world's most powerful military machine – the Red Army and Red Air Force. During the 1930s, Stalin built an Army and Air Force that had more tanks and aircraft than the combined forces of Germany, France, Britain, America, and Japan. It was composed of tens of thousands of high-speed tanks and ground-attack aircraft. It was designed for a lightning surprise attack. To control the Soviet Union and a conquered Europe, Stalin built the largest, most pervasive, and tyrannical political and police apparatus in the history of the world – the CPSU and the NKVD. From the first Five-Year Plan in 1929, this program never changed; the Soviet Union became and remained to the end a giant war machine.

At secret meetings in the pre-war years, Stalin had often discussed his plan for "liberating" a war-torn Europe with the Red Army. The plan always involved getting a war started in Europe in which the Soviet Union would remain neutral until the adversaries had exhausted each other. At that point the Red Army would sweep into Europe to "liberate" the masses. Stalin had written:

> "A great deal depends upon whether we succeed in delaying the war, which is unavoidable, with the capitalist world, until that moment when the capitalists start fighting among themselves." I. V. Stalin, *Sochineniya*, Vol.10, p. 228.
>
> Cited by Viktor Suvorov, *ICEBREAKER*, London, Hamish Hamilton,1990, p. 33.

> "Struggles, conflicts and wars among our enemies are … our greatest ally. If war does break out, we will not sit with folded arms – we will have to take to the field, but we will be the last to do so. And we shall do so in order to throw the decisive load on the scale and tip the balance." I. V. Stalin, *Sochineniya*, Vol. 7, (Moscow, 1952), pp. 14, 27.
>
> Cited by Richard Pipes, *COMMUNISM*, New York, The Modern Library, 2001, p.74.

The decision to finally implement this plan was reached at a special session of the Politburo held on August 19, 1939.

"The question of war or peace is entering a phase which for us is critical. If we conclude the Treaty of Mutual Assistance with France and Great Britain, Germany will renounce its claim to Poland and seek a *modus vivendi* with the Western powers. The war will be set aside, but subsequently events could take on a dangerous character for the USSR. If we accept Germany's offer for the conclusion of a non-aggression pact, she will naturally attack Poland and the entry of France and Great Britain into the war will become inevitable. Western Europe will be caught up in serious troubles and disorders. In these conditions, we shall have good chances to stay outside the conflict, and we may expect our entry into the war to be favorable for us."

"The experience of the past twenty years demonstrates that in time of peace the Communist movement in Europe has no chance of being strong enough to seize power. The dictatorship of the Communist Party may be envisaged only as a result of a great war."

"Thus, our task consists in making sure that Germany should be involved in war as long as possible, so that England and France would be so exhausted that they would no longer be capable of presenting a threat to a Soviet Germany. We shall maintain a position of neutrality, while biding our time; the USSR will grant aid to present-day Germany to provide raw materials and general supplies."

"For these plans to be realized, it is indispensable to prolong the war as long as possible, and it is in this precise direction that we should guide all the forces with which we shall act in Western Europe and in the Balkans."

"Comrades! It is in the interest of the USSR - the Fatherland of the Workers - that war should break out between the Reich and the Franco-British capitalist bloc. We must do everything so that the war should last as long as possible with the aim of weakening both sides. It is for these reasons that we must give priority to the approval of the conclusion of the pact proposed by Germany, and to work so that this war, which will be declared within a few days, shall last as long as possible."

Excerpts from speech of I. V. Stalin to the Plenum of the Politburo of the Central Committee of the All-Union Communist Party, 19 August 1939. Cited by Brian Crozier, *THE RISE AND FALL OF THE SOVIET EMPIRE,* Appendix A.

News of the Politburo meeting and what had been decided quickly leaked out to the Western press. The French news agency Havas published a report of the proceedings. This obviously touched a raw nerve in the Kremlin. Stalin quickly and uncharacteristically published a scathing denial in *Pravda* on November 30, 1939:

"THE FALSE REPORT ISSUED BY THE HAVAS AGENCY"

"The editor of *Pravda* has put the following question to Comrade Stalin. What is Comrade Stalin's attitude to the message issued by the Havas agency on 'Stalin's speech', allegedly made by him 'in the Politburo of 19 August', at which ideas were supposedly advanced to the effect that 'the war must be continued for as long as needed to exhaust the belligerent countries'?

Comrade Stalin has sent the following answer:

'This report issued by the Havas agency, like many more of its messages, is nonsense. I of course cannot know in precisely which nightclub these lies were fabricated. But no matter how many lies the gentlemen of the Havas agency might tell, they cannot deny that:

a) it was not Germany which attacked France and Britain, but France and Britain which attacked Germany, thereby taking upon themselves the responsibility for the present war;

b) after hostilities began, Germany made peace proposals to France and Britain, while the Soviet Union openly supported these German peace proposals, for it considered, and continues to consider, that only as early end to the war as possible can bring relief in a fundamental way to the condition of all countries and all peoples;

c) the ruling circles in Britain and France rejected out of hand both the German peace proposals and the Soviet Union's efforts to end the war as quickly as possible.

Such are the facts. What can the nightclub politicians of the Havas agency provide to counter these facts?'

J. STALIN, *Pravda*, 30 November 1939.

Suvorov, op. cit., p. 43.

During a 1940 meeting with Party agitators in Dnepropetrovsk, Leonid Breshnev was questioned about the Nazi - Soviet Non - Aggression Pact:

"Comrade Breshnev, we have to interpret non - aggression and say that it has to be taken seriously, and that anyone who does not believe in it is talking provocation. But people have little faith in it. So what are we to do? Do we go on interpreting it or not?

Breshnev: "You have to go on interpreting it; and we shall go on interpreting it until not one stone of Nazi Germany remains upon another."

Leonid Breshnev, *Malaya Zemlya*, Moscow, 1978, p. 16.

Suvorov, op. cit., pp. 34, 35.

On March 13, 1940, the Politburo ordered the People's Commissariat for Defense to classify and grade the entire nomenklatura (the ruling elite) of the CPSU, and give them appropriate military ranks in the Red Army and Red Navy. Overnight the Party was converted into a para - military organization.

In March 1939, in a statement to the Eighteenth Congress of the CPSU, Lev Mekhlis, chief of political administration of the Red Army said:

"... If the edge of the second imperialist war should turn against the first socialist state of the world, we must carry military hostilities into the enemy's territory, perform our international duty and increase the number of Soviet republics ... ."

K. Voroshilov, L. Mekhlis, S. Budyonny, G. Stern, *The Red Army Today,* Speeches Delivered at the Eighteenth Congress of the CPSU (B), March 10-21, 1939 (Moscow: Foreign Languages Publishing House, 1939), p. 42.

This is how Red Air Force General Baidukov described future war in *Pravda*:

"What joy and happiness will shine in the faces of those who will receive here in the Great Kremlin Palace the last republic into the brotherhood of nations of the whole world! I envisage clearly the bomber planes destroying the enemy's factories, railway junctions, bridges, depots and positions; low-flying assault aircraft attacking columns of troops and artillery positions with a hail of gunfire; and assault landing ships putting their divisions ashore in the heart of the enemy's dispositions. The powerful and formidable air force of the Land of the Soviets, along with the infantry and tank and artillery troops will do their sacred duty and will help the enslaved peoples to escape from their executioners."

Pravda, Georgi Baidukov, 18 August 1940.

Suvorov, op. cit., p. 352.

On January 1, 1941, *Pravda* greeted the new year with the slogan:

"Let us increase the number of republics of the Soviet Union!"

"Our country is large; the globe must revolve for nine hours before the whole of our vast Soviet land can enter the new year of our victories. The time will come when not nine hours, but all twenty-four hours on the clock will be needed for this to happen ... Who knows where we shall be greeting the new year in five or ten years' time – in what latitude, on what new Soviet meridian?"
Pravda, 1 January 1941.

As the date of Stalin's planned attack drew closer, *Pravda* became more jingoistic:

"Divide our enemies, meet the demand of each of them temporarily and then destroy them one at a time, giving them no opportunity to unite.'
Pravda, 4 March 1941.
Suvorov, op. cit., pp. 35, 36.

On 5 May 1941, Stalin made a speech in the Kremlin honoring the military academy graduates. The speech lasted forty minutes, which for the taciturn Stalin, was tantamount to a filibuster. The speech was not published at that time, but was frequently referenced; more of it was published later.

"At one time or another we have followed a line based on defense....But now that our army has been recon-structed and we have become strong, it is necessary to shift from defense to offense. While securing defense in our country, we must act in an offensist (nastupatel'nym) way. Our military policy must change from defense (oborona) to waging offensist actions. We need to instill in our indoctrination, our propaganda and agitation,

and in our press an offensist spirit. The Red Army is a modern army. It is an army that is offensist."
  A. N. Yakolev, ed., *1941 god. Dokumenty*, Moscow: Mezhdunarodniy Fond "Demokratiya", 1998, p. 162.
  Cited by Albert L. Weeks in *Stalin's Other War,* Appendix 1, pp. 84, 94, 167.
  "J. V. Stalin, the Secretary-General of the CPSU (b), in the course of a speech he made at a reception for the graduates of military academies on 5 May 1941, gave it clearly to be understood that the German Army was the most probable enemy."
  VIZH No. 4 1978, p. 85.
  Suvorov, op. cit., p. 173.

  "...to be ready, on the orders of the High Command, to deliver swift blows utterly to destroy the enemy, to carry out combat operations over his territory and seize important positions.".."the war with Germany will not begin before 1942."
  V. A. Anfilov, *Bessermertnyii povig,* Moscow Nauka 1971, p. 171.
  Suvorov, op. cit., p. 182-183.

By May and June 1941, it was no longer possible to conceal the massive Soviet troop build-up. But it was possible to conceal the date of the planned attack, which is why Stalin permitted the 1942 date to leak out.
  On 8 May 1941, three days after Stalin's secret speech, TASS broadcast an outraged denial of a Japanese news-agency report of a massive build-up of Red Army forces on the western front:
  "Japanese newspapers are publishing reports issued by the *Domei Tsusin Agency* in which it states that the Soviet Union is concentrating strong military forces

on its western frontiers....In this connection, pas-
senger traffic along the Trans-Siberian Railway has
been stopped, so that troops from the Far East can be
transferred mainly to its western frontiers." *TASS* is
authorized to state that this suspiciously strident *Domei
Tsusin* report...is the fruit of the sick imagination of its
authors....

Suvorov, op. cit., p. 188.

On May 15,1941, the People's Commissar of Defense,
Timoshenko and the Chief of the General Staff of the
Red Army, Zhukov sent a memorandum to Stalin titled
"Consideration of the Plan for the Strategic Deployment of the
Armed Forces in Case of War with Germany and Its Allies."
The following are excerpts from the memorandum:

"Taking into account the fact that at the present time
Germany can maintain its army in mobilized readiness
together with its deployed forces in the rear, it has the
capability of preempting us in deploying and mounting a
surprise strike."

"In order to prevent this from happening while destroying the German army, I consider it necessary that
in no way should we yield the initiative for starting hostilities to the German command."

"We should preempt (upridit') the enemy by deploying and attacking the German Army at the very
moment when it has reached the stage of deploying (in
order to wage an attack) but has not yet organized itself
into a front or concentrated all units of its armed forces
along the front...."

"In order that the above may be carried out in the way
indicated, it is necessary in timely fashion to take the
following measures without which it will not be possible
to deliver a surprise strike against the enemy both from

the air as well as from the ground." (There follows a list of measures relating to the locations along the Western Front for deploying Red Army infantry, tank, etc., divisions and the number of days or weeks the various measures will take to execute the Red Army's "surprise strike.")

Yakovlev, op. cit., pp. 215-220.
Weeks, op. cit., Appendix 2, pp. 169-170.

For months prior to the outbreak of hostilities on June 22nd, the Soviets had been engaged in a massive concentration of forces in a huge westward projecting bulge. Ernst Topitsch elegantly described the situation in *Stalin's War*:

"Further indications of the Soviet plan of action are given by the great concentrations of motorized and tank units in and behind the front lines, which protruded so as to form a bulge around Bialstok and Lemberg. About this General Halder correctly commented at a later hearing in Nuremberg: 'No troops deployed for defense would be concentrated in such numbers in an area projecting into the enemy.' This has since been confirmed from Soviet sources. Marshal Schukov reported that the decision to concentrate troops in the Bialstok area had already been made in 1940, and on this decisive point Major-General Grigorenko spoke quite frankly:

"More than half the troops of our Western Military Region were in the area round Bialstok and to the west of that, that is, in an area which projected into enemy territory. There could only be one reason for such a distribution, namely, that these troops were intended for a surprise offensive. In the event of an enemy attack these troops would already be half encircled. The enemy would only need to deal a few short blows at the base of our wedge and the encirclement would be complete."

"Here the intention to attack is portrayed without any shadow of doubt; the Soviet failure was due to their belief that their own counter-attack would prevent the Germans from achieving such an encirclement. Regarding the bulge in the front around Lemberg there is evidence of even greater authority, Marshal Bagramian, who at the outbreak of war was a colonel and in charge of operations in the Kiev Special Military Region and therefore familiar with the situation, wrote about it as follows:"

"The area protruding towards the west, including such a large town as Lvov, was considered to be a favorite deployment area in case we had to change over to a large-scale attack. It was not by chance that we had concentrated there two of our biggest and most battle-trained mechanized corps, the Fourth and the Eighth."

Ernst Topitsch, *Stalin's War*, p. 106.

In the 1930s, during the first two five-year plans, the Soviet Union had built an impregnable line of fortifications, comparable to the Maginot Line, but longer and deeper, that ran from Leningrad to Odessa – it was called the Stalin Line. In the spring of 1941, Stalin began dismantling this powerful line of defense. A defensive line would not be needed if one were planning to launch the greatest offensive operation in history.

"The situation was becoming absurd. When we were faced by weak armies of comparatively small countries, our frontiers were really well and truly safe. When Nazi Germany became our neighbor the defensive installations put up by the engineers along the former frontier were abandoned and even partially dismantled."

"At the beginning of May 1941, following Stalin's speech at the reception for military academy graduates,

the brake was applied even more strongly to all work that was being done to build engineered defenses and to lay down mines."
GRU Colonel Ilya Starinov, *Miny Zhdut Svoego Chasa*, p.186.
Suvorov, op. cit., pp.28, 175.
On 13 June 1941, the greatest mass movement of troops in history began. The First Strategic Echelon had 170 divisions; 56 of these were stationed right up against the western frontier. The remaining 114 divisions were in the western districts, a short distance from the frontier. "Between 12 and 15 June, the western military districts were ordered to move all divisions in the interior of the country into positions close to the state frontiers."
V. Khvostov, Major-General A. Grylev, *Kommunist* 1968, No. 12, p.68.

Before May 1941, Soviet newspapers had glorified war in general and happily celebrated Germany's victories in Europe. Pravda waxed poetic about "modern war in all its terrible beauty!"
Pravda, 19 August 1940.
Suvorov, op. cit., p.176.
The day after Stalin's secret May 5th speech, everything suddenly changed:

"The fire of the Second Imperialist War blazes beyond the frontiers of our Motherland. The whole weight of its incalculable misfortunes is laid on the shoulders of the workers. The people do not want war. Their gazes are fixed on the countries of socialism which are reaping the fruits of peaceful labor. They see with every justification a solid bastion for peace in the armed forces

of our Motherland, in the Red Army and Navy. In the present complex international situation it is necessary to be ready for surprises of all kinds...."
Pravda, 6 May 1941, leading article.
Suvorov, op. cit., p.176.

This same terminology prefaced every Soviet "liberation." In May 1941, the whole gigantic communist propaganda apparatus suddenly began sounding the alarm "to be ready for unexpected events." The People's Commissar for Defense issued order No. 191 to "all companies, batteries, squadrons, air squadrons and on ships"..."to be ready for unexpected events."

General S. P. Ivanov, Chief of the General Staff Academy of the Armed Forces of the USSR, and a group of leading Soviet historians, produced a comprehensive study entitled The Initial Period of the War *(Nachalnye Period Voiny.)* The study indicated that Red Army westward troop movements began in February, were increased in March, reached enormous proportions in April and May, and became a flood in June. The full build-up of Soviet forces on the German frontier was planned to be complete by July 10th. The railroads were paralyzed for almost six months by these secret military movements.

There were many indications that the planned launch date for Soviet Operation GROZA (Thunderstorm) was 6 July 1941. Zhukov and Stalin liked to launch surprise attacks on Sunday mornings, and 6 July 1941 was the last Sunday before the concentration of Soviet forces would have been complete. Soviet military doctrine dictated that an offensive should begin before the concentration of troops was completed.

The study not only admitted that Hitler launched a preventive attack, but also put a time to it: "the Nazi command

succeeded in forestalling our troops literally in the last two weeks before the war began."
General of the Army S. P. Ivanov, *Nachalnyi Period Voiny*, Moscow *Voenizdat* 1974. pp. 211-212.
Suvorov, op. cit., pp. 206, 327.
Dr. Albert L. Weeks, author *Stalin's Other War, Soviet Grand Strategy 1939-1941 and Lend-Lease Aid to the USSR in World War II* has informed this author of two newly published works by Russian historians (in Russian). Both support the thesis concerning Stalin's prewar offencist war plans. The first, by Mark Solonin, *Bochka Obruchi (Barrel Stays, or How the Great Patriotic War Began)*, 2004, provides thorough documentation for the Soviet offensive military buildup, weapon by weapon, on the Eastern Front before Hitler's attack in June 1941.

The second book, by military historian Vladimir Beshanov, *Tankovoy Pogrom 1941 goda (The Tank Massacre of 1941)*, published in Minsk, 2004, gives a systematic, detailed analysis of Soviet war-planning as it looked by spring 1941. The author shows that Stalin was planning his own disarming attack against the Wehrmacht.

A third book by Viktor Suvorov, author of the watershed study, *Icebreaker*, is near completion. It is said to provide additional proof of Stalin's offensive-war plans.

These books together with Weeks's study should convince any doubters about Stalin's offensive war plans or those who have been misled in the past by books following the Soviet line on the "Great Patriotic War": that Stalin was an innocent bystander or passive victim of one-sided aggression emanating from Germany alone.

THE GREAT TERROR (1934 -1938)

In the middle of this massive campaign to industrialize and arm the Soviet Union. Stalin set about to gain absolute control of everything. What followed has been called The Great Purge or The Great Terror. In the early 1930s, Stalin had told Yagoda that he preferred people to support him out of fear rather than conviction; conviction can change. The CPSU was completely cauterized of Stalin's opponents during the Purge period. Fewer than two percent of the delegates to the 1934 XVII Party Congress returned to the 1939 XVIII Party Congress, the other 98% had been executed or shipped to the Gulag.

December 1, 1934, marked the starting date of an avalanche of terror. On that day Sergei M. Kirov was murdered in his Smolny office, headquarters of the CPSU in Leningrad. Kirov was the Party Secretary of Leningrad; Leningrad was Russia's "window on Europe"; the most civilized and culturally advanced city in the country. Kirov was the prize orator of the Party; the best since Trotsky. Kirov was charismatic and approachable; Kirov was a Russian; Stalin was a Georgian. Kirov's popularity was growing; he was the rising star of the Party. At the XVII Party Congress in January 1934, a group of senior delegates surreptitiously tried to persuade Kirov to run against Stalin for the post of General Secretary of the Party. To Stalin that was tantamount to a death sentence.

Kirov was supposedly killed by Leonard Nikolaev, a 30 year old unemployed metalworker; a Party cipher. The NKVD first concocted a story that Nikolaev killed Kirov because Kirov was having an affair with his wife, Milda Draule, another Party cipher. Kirov was a womanizer, but with a taste for beautiful ballerinas; not working-class Milda Draules. All this quickly became irrelevant when the NKVD decided to make Nikolaev a member of a terrorist organization affiliated with the so-called "Leningrad Centre." On the day of the murder, under orders from Stalin, the Secretary of the Presidium signed an antiterrorist decree, which provided for the summary execution of anyone making an attempt on the life of a Soviet official.

Almost everyone, including Khruschev, now agree that Stalin masterminded the plot to kill Kirov, as an excuse to wipe out all potential opposition to his absolute control of the Party and the Soviet Union The official, but false, version of Kirov's assassination, given by Stalin, was the following:

> "The investigation established that in 1933 and 1934 an underground counter-revolutionary terrorist group had been formed in Leningrad consisting of former members of the Zinoviev opposition and headed by a so-called "Leningrad Centre." The purpose of this group was to murder leaders of the Communist Party. S. M. Kirov was chosen as the first victim. The testimony of the members of this counter-revolutionary group showed that they were connected with representatives of foreign capitalist states and were receiving funds from them."

> "Soon afterwards the existence of an underground counter-revolutionary organization called the 'Moscow Centre' was discovered. The preliminary investigation and the trial revealed the villainous part played by Zinoviev, Kamenev, Yevdokimov and other leaders of this organization in cultivating the terrorist mentality

among their followers, and in plotting the murder of members of the party Central Committee and the Soviet Government."
History of the Communist Party of the Soviet Union (Bolsheviks), Short Course, New York: International Publishers, 1939, p. 326.

Based on this version of the assassination, a secret trial against the Zinoviev- Kamenev group was staged in January 1935; all defendants were sentenced to prison. Although the Great Purge began with the arrest of former opposition members, it soon spread to every level of Soviet society, from workers and peasants, to high Party officials and the military establishment.

On May 13.1935. the Central Committee of the CPSU ordered a "renewal of membership cards." This was tantamount to a purge of the party. The purge operation lasted for four years and resulted in the arrest, trial, and execution of millions of Party members as well as non-Communists. There was hardly a Party unit, a state enterprise, an administrative unit, or a scientific or cultural institution that was not decimated by it. The Purge swept through the highest echelons of the military, the secret police, the universities, industry, trade unions; no one was left untouched. On April 7, 1935, a decree extended all punishment, including the death sentence, down to twelve-year-olds. Stalin could now legally threaten the lives of the children of anyone not cooperating with the NKVD.

The bloody holocaust started with the appointment of a special "Commission" to watch over the NKVD and the Purge operation. The "Commission" was headed by the "dreadful dwarf" (five foot) Nikolai I. Yezhov, a tiny, slim man, who was said to have an "old dwarf's face".

"...In these investigations a certain Yezhov, an ex-workman, particularly distinguished himself...His creed was quite simple: Stalin was the greatest genius in all human history, and the Russian people were a marvel...but anyone who came between Stalin and the people was entirely worthless and must be shot.

He was filled with an almost morbid hatred of the intelligentsia, and he had his reason for this. Poor Yezhov, who now became a gigantic incubus, a blood-thirsty figure looming over all Russia, had one weak spot–his wife....To his misfortune the lady was something of a literary snob, moving in all the literary circles of Moscow; here it was that she found her lovers. These circles were closely associated with the intellectuals in the party, and to Yezhov both sets were equally odious. The man was in torment, and as time went on he became an embittered enemy of all educated people. In his view they were capable of any wickedness and any treachery, filled with infinite cunning."
Nikolaus Basseches, *Stalin,* New York: E. P. Dutton & Co., 1952, pp.274, 275.

During the course of the Purge, Party members were invited to "reveal" and "expose" their comrades; a flood of denunciation, usually from persons seeking to save their necks or advance their careers, inundated the Party committees and the NKVD.

"The zeal with which young people and subordinates strove to "unmask" and accuse their seniors was particularly noteworthy. Students "unmasked" their professors, humble party members denounced those in official positions, junior officials accused those above them...."

F. Beck W. Godin, *Russian Purge and the Extraction of Confession,* New York: The Viking Press, 1951, pp. 24,25.

The vast spy network, which had been growing since the early Soviet years, now assumed incredible proportions. Tens of thousands of so-called seksots (sekretnyi sotrudnik, meaning secret collaborators) were recruited and planted throughout the Soviet Union. It was estimated that every fifth person in the average office was a seksot. The seksots:

"...were to be found throughout the population. It was as good as certain that the messengers, chauffeurs, secretaries, and translators of everybody who occupied any sort of leading position in the political or economic administration, the Army, or the NKVD, were seksots. They had to report on their superiors and their superiors' families at regular intervals. The opinions, the private life, the social contacts of every person of any importance in the Soviet Union were constantly spied and reported on from several quarters at the same time, and the reports were checked with one another."
Beck and Godin, *op. cit.,* pp. 164, 165.

During the purge period, almost every Soviet citizen was compelled in one way or another, often by entrapment, to inform on friends, neighbors, or fellow workers. A joke of the period, defined a decent Soviet citizen as someone who behaved like a swine, but didn't enjoy it.

A 1936 CPSU directive demanded that members "see through and expose" enemies of the Party no matter how well disguised. To prove a member's political vigilance, a norm (quota) of one hundred denunciations per member was proposed. This led to Stakhanovite denouncers like comrade

Polia Nikilenko, a Kiev party apparatchik, who Khrushchev said denounced over 8000 people; most of whom were executed. Stalin proclaimed her "heroine" of the Party. In Kiev, the streets would empty whenever comrade Nikilenko was spotted; the people were terrified of even being seen by her.

In 1938, NKVD official Zakovski was brought in by Stalin to invigorate the purges. An extremely brutal man, Zakovski bragged that he could make Marx confess to being an agent of Bismark. Zakovski ordered a norm (quota) of 200 arrests per day.

Vladimir Petrov, who defected in 1954, while a Soviet spy-chief in Australia, had this to say about his work in the 1936 to 1938 period:

> "I handled hundreds of signals to all parts of the Soviet Union which were couched in the following form:
> 'To N.K.V.D., Frunze. You are charged with the task of exterminating 10,000 enemies of the people. Report results by signal. – Yezhov.'
> "And in due course the reply would come back:"
> 'In reply to yours of such-and-such date, the following enemies of the Soviet people have been shot.'"
> Vladimir Petrov and Evodkia, Empire of Fear, Praeger, NYC, 1956.
> Cited by Rummell, op. cit., p. 2

In September 1936, Stalin decided to get rid of Yagoda as chief of the NKVD and appoint Yezhov in his place. Yagoda was transferred to another post; later he was arrested, tried, and executed. Stalin plotted a course of unlimited terror. Yezhov became its living symbol; his 26 months in office went down in Soviet history as the era of "Yezhovschina." Yezhov first purged the NKVD. Any personnel who had shown any signs of humanity and compassion in the past were exterminated. They were replaced by sociopathic "Clockwork Orange" thugs; brutality courses were initiated.

"A partial list ofYezhov's victims includes almost all the eighty members of the Soviet Council of War created in 1934; the majority of the members of Stalin's own Central Committee and his Control Commission; most of the members of the Executive Committee of the Soviets, of the Council of People's Commissars, of the Council of Labor and Defense, of the leaders of the Communist International; all of the chiefs and deputy chiefs of the Ogpu; a host of ambassadors and other diplomats; the heads of all the regional and autonomous republics of the Soviet Union; 35,000 members of the officers' corps; almost the entire staff of *Pravda* and *Izvestia;* a great number of writers, musicians, and theater directors; and finally a majority of the leaders of the Young Communist League, the cream of the generation from whom the greatest loyalty to Stalin was expected."
W. G. Krivitsky, *In Stalin's Secret Service, NYC,* Harper & Bros., 1939, p.177.

The objective of the arrests, interrogations, and trials was to extract "confessions." To Stalin and the NKVD, a confession was incontestable proof of guilt. Every arrested person had to be made to confess and plead guilty; fictitious confessions were standard.

"Everyone was required to denounce at least one other person who had "recruited" him, i.e, had persuaded him to engage in counter-revolutionary activity and had directed him. Everyone was also required to denounce as many other people as possible whom he himself had recruited and induced to commit political crimes, or who had worked with him in the same counter-revolutionary

organization. Again and again during the hour-long and
often day-long interrogations, the prisoner was asked,
"Who recruited you?" and "Whom did you recruit?"

Beck and Godin, *op. cit.,* pp. 45, 46.

NKVD working hours were unlimited; interrogations
usually lasted through the night. The NKVD had no
regular executioners; any NKVD man could be called
upon at any time to execute the "sentenced" prisoner.
Stalin made everyone an accomplice. After being sum-
marily dispatched with a bullet to the back of the head,
the bodies were carted off to mass graves in NKVD vans
ghoulishly marked "Meat."

"In the office of every prosecuting investigator the
most important article of furniture is his couch. For
the character of his work is such that it often keeps
him going at consecutive stretches of twenty to forty
hours. He is himself almost as much a captive as the
prisoners. His duties know no limits. They may extend
from grilling prisoners to shooting them. For it is one
of the peculiarities of the Soviet judicial process that
despite the tremendous numbers of executions, there are
no regular executioners. Sometimes the men who go
down to the cellar to carry out the death decrees of the
collegiums of the Ogpu are officers and sentries of the
building. Sometimes they are the investigators and pros-
ecutors themselves. For an analogy to this, one must try
to imagine a New York District Attorney obtaining a first
degree murder conviction and rushing up to Sing Sing to
throw the switch in the death chamber."

Kravitsky, *op. cit.,* p. 145.

An exception to this policy was V. M. Blothin, Stalin's
granite-faced top executioner. He was usually assisted by two

brothers: Vasily and Ivan Zhigarov. Blothin wore a leather butcher's apron during executions. At Katyn Forest, Blothin and the Zhigarov brothers killed 7000 Polish officers in 28 nights, setting themselves a quota of 250 a night. They used German Walther PPK pistols to mislead any investigators.

Confessions were extracted by threats, beatings, torture, and promises, rarely kept, of leniency or freedom. Stalin advised to "beat, beat, and beat again." Prisoners were sometimes beaten so hard, their eyes literally popped out of their heads; often, they were gouged out. Prisoners were routinely beaten to death; such deaths being recorded as heart attacks. Torturing prisoners was made obligatory by a special 1937 instruction. The Purge reached far down into the bureaucracy and throughout the economy. Plant managers, engineers, scientists, teachers, poets – the full spectrum of the technical and cultural intelligentsia – were caught up in the NKVD dragnets. Very few of the arrested were ever given any sort of trial. There were four main prisons in Moscow for "politicals": Butyrki, Lubyanka, Lefortovo, and Sukhanovka. Sukhanovka, originally St. Catherine's Nunnery, was called "the dacha." Prisoners at Sukhanovka were tortured continually. Solzhenitsyn said anyone sent there was either driven insane, could thereafter talk only disconnected nonsense, or were killed.

"The so-called purges of the 1930s were a terror campaign that in indiscriminate ferocity and number of victims had no parallel in world history. It was minutely supervised by Stalin himself, whose instructions to the local authorities focused on one method: beat them until they confess to crimes they have not committed." "At the pinnacle of the Great Terror, the Politburo issued 'quotas' to the police authorities, instructing them as to what percentage of the population in their district was to be shot and what percentage sent to camps."

Richard Pipes, *COMMUNISM,* New York, The Modern Library, 2001, pp.62-64.

Four great "Moscow Show Trials" were held between August 1936 and March 1938, which ended in the execution of most of the old Bolsheviks. The standard charges were espionage for a foreign power, "diversion" and sabotage, conspiring against the Soviet regime, and plots to kill the Soviet leaders. The prosecutor was Andrei Vyshinsky, who demanded the death sentence in every case. The Zinoviev–Kamenev trial was staged in August 1936; the sixteen defendants were:

"...accused of treason, of espionage, of terrorist intrigues, of intelligence with the enemy, of collusion with the fascists, of monstrous, unintelligible and impossible crimes. They confessed everything; they accused instead of defending themselves; they denounced each other and ardently vindicated Stalin."

Boris Souvarine, *Stalin,* (New York, Alliance Book Corp., Longmans, Green & Co.. 1939). p. 626.

All sixteen defendants were sentenced to death and executed within 24 hours. During the trial, Mikhail Tomski, another old companion of Lenin and head of the Soviet trade unions, committed suicide. There was a flood of suicides during the purges, a large number of prominent leaders and writers took their own lives. Exactly six days after Zinoviev, Kamenev and all the other defendants of the first trial had been executed, Stalin ordered Yagoda and Yezhov to select 5000 more members of the former opposition who were being held in the Gulag. They were executed in secret.

During the Trials, Old Bolshevik Budu Mdivani said: "You are telling me Stalin has promised to spare the lives of Old Bolsheviks! I have known Stalin for thirty years. Stalin won't rest until he has butchered all of us, beginning with the unweaned baby and ending with the blind great-grandmother!"

Alexander Orlov, *THE SECRET HISTORY OF STALIN'S CRIMES,* London, 1954, p. 249.

In the Great Terror, Stalin massacred Lenin's Party.

Stalin and Yezhov usually spent three or four hours a day pouring over lists of potential victims. Only the most senior people were screened by Stalin and Yezhov; the fate of millions of ordinary citizens was decided by junior level NKVD. Stalin is known to have personally approved of 383 lists containing approximately 44,000 names slated for execution.

Nikita S. Khrushchev, "Secret Report," cited by Bertram G. Wolfe, *KHRUSHCHEV and STALIN'S GHOST:* p.154.

Prisons became packed; camps filled with millions of newcomers. Certain categories of people were automatically condemned. Rail workers were always Japanese spies, engineers were saboteurs, historians were terrorists. Estimates of the numbers arrested and shipped to the Gulag soared.

"The insane momentum resulted in `street sweeps` in which everyone who happened to be on the street at a given moment was swept away to the gulag."

Paul Craig Roberts, Nightmare on film, *The Washington Times,* 8/3/03.

"...Calculations of this kind were often made by the prisoners, usually with the help of State attorneys and NKVD officials confined in the same cell. These showed that the number arrested during the Yezhov period must have been from five to ten percent of the entire population. Assuming the population of the Soviet Union to have been about 150,000,000, this points to a total of at least 7,000,000 to 14,000,000 prisoners and people living in detention under the NKVD. The figure includes victims of the former purges, including kulaks not released up to 1938....The proportion also varied in different classes and occupation groups. The proportion of arrests among the intelligentsia, railway workers, and Red Army officers was substantially above the average."

Beck and Godin, *op. cit.,* pp. 70,71

"...In June reverberated the thunderbolt which decapitated the General Staff and struck terror into the country: under the unheard-of charge of espionage, under the ridiculous pretext of having "violated their military oath, betrayed their country, betrayed the peoples of the U.S.S.R., betrayed the Red Army," Marshal Tukhachevsky, Generals Yakir, Kork, Uborevich, Eideman, Feldman, Primakov and Putna, all well-known "heroes of the Civil War," all several times decorated with the Order of the Red Flag, all classed as adversaries of Trotsky and partisans of Stalin, were tried *in camera,* condemned to death without witnesses or defense, and executed within forty-eight hours."

Souvarine, *op. cit.,* p. 629.

Between June 1937 and the autumn of 1938, Stalin ordered the execution of:

All 11 Vice Commissars of Defense
98 out of 100 members of the Supreme Military Soviet
3 out of the 5 Marshals
13 out of the 15 Army Commanders
8 out of the 9 Fleet Admirals and Admirals Grade 1
50 out of 57 Corps Commanders
154 out of 186 Divisional Commanders
16 out 16 Army Commissars
25 out of 28 Corps Commissars
58 out of 64 Divisional Commissars
Robert Conquest, *The Great Terror,* New York, Oxford University Press, 1990, p.450.

At the rate the arrests were being made in mid-1938 almost the entire urban population would have been implicated in a few months. Had the purges continued at the same pace, the chaos would have destroyed the nation. Stalin had to ease the pressure. He had achieved his goals; he had destroyed his old opponents; instilled unqualified terror in any potential opponents; gained absolute control of Soviet society and the apparatus of the State. Now he had to find scapegoats to blame for the whole disaster. Stalin had always been very successful in making the people believe the NKVD operated independently of the Kremlin. There was a story that when Ehrenburg and Pastenak met on the street during the Terror, they lamented: "If only someone would tell Stalin."

In July 1938, Stalin appointed a fellow Georgian, Lavrenti Beria, as deputy to Yezhov; in December, Beria took over the NKVD. Yezhov disappeared without a trial or a trace. Thousands of Yezhov's and Yagoda's personnel were arrested and executed for their over-zealous excesses.

Beria executed nearly all top NKVD officers and shipped most of the lower ranks off to the Gulag. Beria deftly handled the problem this way:

"He invited the Ministers of the Interior of all the republics and all the higher Cheka officials who had especially distinguished themselves during the purges to a conference in Moscow. Having been asked to leave their weapons in the cloakroom, they were received in the banqueting hall with lavish hospitality. Everybody was in excellent spirits when Beria appeared. Instead of the expected address he uttered just one sentence: 'You are under arrest.' They were led from the hall and shot in the cellar the same night."

Bernhard Roeder, Katorga: An Aspect of Modern Slavery. Translated by Lionel Kochan, Heinemann, London, 1958. Cited by Rummell, op. cit., p. 113.

Stalin was "shocked" – "shocked" to discover such horrible things had been going on behind his back.

As you read about Sukhanovka and Kalima, try to imagine what it must have been like to have been a prisoner. It is impossible, but try to feel their unrelenting pain and suffering. Try to imagine working at Kalima, where your health was destroyed in three weeks. It was the State's plan to literally work you to death in three months.

Try to imagine yourself a prisoner at Sukhanovka. At Sukhanovka, the beatings never stopped. You were never permitted to sleep. The shrieks and screams never stopped. Every square millimeter of a prisoner's body was wracked with unbearable pain; but the beatings never stopped. The prisoner's heads were stuffed in great buckets of excrement, urine, and vomit; then the beatings were resumed. The shrieks and screams never stopped. Every prisoner who entered Sukhanovka was either killed or driven mad. Try to imagine what kind of unspeakable sub-human could spend every working day of his career committing such atrocities. This was how the Vanguard built the Worker's Paradise.

TANKS

During the 1930s Stalin created an armaments industry that was beyond the wildest imagining of the outside world. The emphasis of the five-year plans was almost entirely on "heavy industry," which was a euphemism for war industry.

"For the period January 1, 1929 to July 1, 1941, capital investment in the industry amounted to 199.5 billion rubles, of which 169.5 billion rubles, i.e., 85 percent, were invested in heavy industry."
Bolshaya Sovietskaya Entsiklopediya, vol. XLIII. (1956), p.562.

According to Professor Albert Weeks, between 1939 and 1941, Red Army manpower grew from under two million to over five million, and from under 100 divisions to over 300. By 1941, the Soviets were producing 12,000 tanks a year. (Weeks, op. cit., p.33.)

According to official Russian sources, *Velikaia Otechestvennaia voina (VOV)*, the Germans launched Barbarossa on 6/22/41 with 4.1 million men in 153 divisions and three brigades, equipped with 4170 tanks, 40,500 guns and mortars, and 3613 combat aircraft. Also, according to *VOV*, by 12/5/41, the Red Army had lost over 20,000 tanks, 17,000 combat aircraft, and 60,000 to 100,000 guns and mortars.

V.A. Zolotarev, ed., *Velikaia Otechestvennaia voina (VOV) 1941-1945*, Kn.1. *The Great Patriotic War 1941-1945, Book 1*. Moscow: *'Nauka' 1998*. Cited by David M. Glantz in *BARBAROSSA,* p. 215 and p. 228.

Weeks put Soviet losses at 22,000 tanks and up to 25,000 aircraft in the first four months. (Weeks, op. cit., p. 114.) For the Red Army to have lost 22,000 tanks, 25,000 planes, and 60,000 to 100,000 guns and mortars in the five months between 6/22/41 and 12/5/41, their overall resources are bound to have been enormous. In *PANZER LEADER*, General Heinz Guderian relates that as a Colonel in 1933, he had visited the giant Soviet Komintern locomotive works in Kharkov, where in addition to locomotives, the plant was producing twenty-two Christie/Russki-type (BTs) tanks a day, as a sideline. Operating five days a week, they would have produced approximately 5700 tanks per year. If the Russians had continued production at this rate for the next eight years, by 1941 they would have produced 45,000 tanks at the Kharkov plant alone. The Soviets were also producing tanks at the Kirov plant in Leningrad, the Nizhniy Tagil plant in the Urals, and the Dzerhezinsky Tractor Works in Stalingrad. During the first two Five-Year Plans (1928-1938), the Soviets built more than thirty tank factories.

The Dzerhezinsky Tractor Works was the pride of Soviet industry. It was built in eleven months and opened on May Day 1931. It was a mile long and contained ten miles of railroad track. Obviously, during the 1930s, the Soviets had the capacity to produce at Leningrad, Stalingrad, and Nazhniy Tagil a very large number of tanks. In 1936, it was announced that the Osoaviachim had trained 900,000 military drivers. It was estimated that the number of tractors in the Soviet Union increased from 100,000 in 1930 to 500,000 in 1937; 176,000 were produced in 1937. There were about fifteen tractor factories in the Soviet Union during this period. Tank factories and tractor factories could be readily adapted to produce either type vehicle.

If the Russians were producing over 5000 tanks a year just at the Kharkov plant in 1933, and if they built over 30 tank factories and 15 tractor factories in the 1930s, then their tank production potential was staggering. You could pick almost any number you like for their total tank strength in 1941 – 30,000, 40,000, 50,000, whatever. We know for example, that the Kirov plant produced 1225 T- 34s between June 1940 and June 1941 – the first year of production, when you are still trying to iron-out production problems. T-34s were also being built at Stalingrad.

The great Kirov plant in Leningrad was moved to Chelybinsk in the winter of 1941. It was rebuilt next to the huge tank plant that had been moved from Kharkov. This complex became known as Tankograd; it produced the heavy KV tank and later the powerful Josef Stalin tank. Part of the Kharkov plant was grafted on to the Nizhniy Tagil plant in the Urals. It became known as Uralmash zavod. It and the Dzerzinsky plant produced the T- 34s. Even after these massive relocations of the Soviet tank industry in 1941, they produced over 25,000 tanks in 1942; 13,500 of these were T- 34s. Between 1941 and 1943, Russian tanks were produced at 42 factories in Central Russia, the Urals, Leningrad, Stalingrad, and Kharkov. In 1942, the Stalingrad plant produced 5475 tanks.

In May 1940, Germany was producing 125 tanks of all types per month – 1500 per year. After the 1940 campaign, Hitler ordered tank production to be increased to 800 to 1000 tanks per month – 9000 to 12,000 per year. But the Wehrmacht Ordnance Office talked him out of it, saying it would cost two billion Reichmarks and require 100,000 skilled specialist workers. By 1942, German production had been upped to 600 tanks per month – 7200 per year. Other sources have put German tank production at 3256 in 1941 and 4278 in 1942. The Wehrmacht was not a motorized army. The pace of Barbarossa was set by horse-drawn vehicles; 750,000 horses took part in the attack. Of the Wehrmacht's 153 attacking divisions, 119 had horse-drawn vehicles.

It seemed to the Germans in 1941 that the Russians never ran out of tanks, aircraft, or men. According to Chief of Army High Command (OKH) General Halder, the Germans had originally estimated that the Russians had about the same number of divisions as they had – around 200. But by August 1941, they had already identified 360 Russian divisions on the Eastern Front; there were also 30 divisions facing the Japanese in Manchuria.

In a meeting with Harry Hopkins on July 31, 1941, Stalin told Hopkins that the Red Army had 60 tank divisions with 350 to 400 tanks each. He also told Hopkins that each Russian infantry division had 50 tanks. As noted above, by August 1941, the German High Command had already identified 360 Russian divisions on the Eastern Front. This meant that by Stalin's admission, the Red Army had between 21,000 and 24,000 tanks in their armored divisions. It would also mean that their 300-odd infantry divisions had another 15,000 tanks. This means that using Stalin's numbers, which are almost certain to have been understated, inasmuch as he was asking Hopkins for massive American aid, the Red Army had between 36,000 and 39,000 tanks in June 1941. Even with the massive disruptions and relocations, Stalin told Hopkins they were currently producing 1000 tanks and 1800 planes per month. He also said Russian planes were better than the German planes.

Conference between M. Stalin and Harry Hopkins, 7/31/41, NARA.

THE CHRISTIE/RUSSKI TANK

In June 1941, the most numerous tank in the Soviet inventory was the BT-7. BT stood for Bystrokhadnii Tank, literally, Fast Tank; a k a, the Christie/Russki Tank. It was based on American J. Walter Christie's T-3 tank. At Fort Meade, Maryland in 1929, the T-3 ran an obstacle course of eight-inch felled logs and four feet deep mud at 30 mph. With its tracks on it ran 42.5 mph cross-country; with its removable tracks off, it sped down the highway at 70 mph. It was powered by a 338 HP Liberty V-12 aircraft engine. In July 1932, Christie demonstrated an improved version powered by a 750 HP Hispano-Suiza engine. It easily rolled through the obstacle course of 24-inch logs and leaped across 12-foot trenches. On its tracks, it raced down the road at 60.5 mph; with its tracks off, it reached 110 mph. Changing tracks took 30 minutes.

U. S. Army Ordnance would not buy Christie's supertank, but the Russians offered him $10,000 a month to come to Russia and take charge of its production. He declined, but later, desperate for money, he sold them a couple of tanks of a design somewhere between the T-3 and the supertank for $150,000. General Heinz Guderian, Germany's leading tank expert, considered Christie the world's greatest tank designer. In 1935, the Germans offered Christie a million dollars to come to Germany and be their chief tank designer. Despite being broke and an outcast in Washington, Christie refused their offer.

For years, Christie's 1932 supertank sat unheralded on a sidewalk beside one of the Smithsonian Institute's building. During World War II, the government refused Christie's constant pleas to let him serve in any capacity. Broke and friendless, "the greatest tank designer who ever lived" died of a broken heart on January 10, 1944, in a small house in Falls Church, Virginia.

The Russians bought Christie's M-1931 (T-3) tank in 1931, and immediately put it production at the Komintern Factory in Kharkov, designating it the BT-1. Between 1932 and 1938, it was continually improved and up-gunned as the BT-2, BT-3, BT-5, BT-7, and BT-8. The BT-1 was equipped with a 37mm gun; the BT-3 through BT-7 with a 45mm L/46 gun; in 1938, the BT-7s and BT-8s were armed with either the 45mm L/46 or the 76.2 L/16.5 infantry support gun. All could operate on their road wheels or tracks; the tracks being easily removed or reinstalled. All their hulls had pyramidally shaped front armor. All BTs were high-speed, lightly-armored "break-through" or "blitzkreig" tanks, designed to operate in the enemy's rear area.

Of the 3200 German tanks that drove into Russia in June 1941, 2068 were Mark IIIs. Of the Mark IIIs, 131 were still armed with 37mm guns, 1893 were equipped with the 50mm L/42 short barreled gun, and only 40 with the 50mm L/60 long barreled gun. All Mark IIIs had a road speed of 25 mph and 30mm of armor on both the hull and turret. The Mark IV weighed about the same as the Mark III, had the same speed and armor protection, and was armed with a short barreled 75mm gun that was comparable to the BTs 76.2mm gun. While the BTs were faster than the Mark IIIs and IVs, the latter were better armored. Also, the German 50mm L/42 was a more powerful gun than the Russian 45mm L/46. A few words about tank guns. A 50mm L/60 means that the length of the barrel is 50mm times 60 or 3000mm. A battleship's 16"/50 gun is 16 inches times 50 or 800 inches long. The object is to hit the enemy's tank with a high-density projectile traveling at the highest possible terminal velocity. To achieve high muzzle velocity (MV), it is desirable to make the tanks guns as long as practicable. This is so the burning propellant gases in the gun barrel have a longer time to exert pressure on the base of the projectile as it travels down the tube. Thus, on a German Mark III equipped with a 50mm L/60 gun, the propellant had approximately 50% longer burn time than a Mark III equipped with a 50mm L/42 gun, and thus imparted a roughly 50% higher MV to the projectile.

The BTs were the tanks you saw in 1930s newsreels, dashing through Red Square on May Day at 60 mph. Production was started in 1931 at the Komintern Factory in Kharkov. The BT could run on either tracks or wheels; the engine and transmission were in the rear; it was driven by the rear sprockets when on tracks or the rear pair of wheels, when on wheels. When on wheels, it was steered by the front pair of wheels; when on tracks, by the conventional brake and clutch method. Until the BT-7 models, it was steered by a steering wheel instead of levers. It was rarely used in the wheeled mode. The suspension was complicated and difficult to maintain, but provided a very stable gun platform.

All BTs had a three man crew. The BT-1 through BT-5 had a top road speed of 69 mph, a cross-country speed of 39 mph, and a cruising speed of 40 mph. BT-1 through BT-5 had hull and turret armor of 13mm. BT-6 was never produced. The BT-7 had a new conical turret up-armored to 15mm and front hull armor increased to 22mm. Its top speed was reduced to 46 mph, cross-country speed to 33 mph, but cruising speed remained at 40 mph. The weight of the BTs were gradually increased from 11 tons on the BT-2 to 13.8 tons on the BT-7. The BT-7M (a k a BT-8) mounted a 45mm L/46 or a 76.2mm L/16.5 infantry support gun and weighed 14.6 tons.

BT-1: Armed with two machine guns (MG); never put in production.

BT-2: Put in production in 1932; armed with a 37mm anti-tank gun.

BT-3&4: Armed with a 45mm L/46 gun, with MV of 2350 fps.

BT-5: Started production end of 1932; new more powerful V/12 350 HP aircraft engine.

BT-7: Started production in 1935; armed with the 45mm L/46 or the 76.2mm L/16.5 infantry support gun. The BT-7 became the most numerous tank model in the Red Army. It was first powered by a 450 HP V/12 gas engine; this was replaced by the famous BD-2 V/12 400 HP aluminum diesel engine; the first aluminum diesel tank engine in the world. A 500 HP version of the BD-2 powered the T-34.

The BTs were the most numerous, but by no means the only tanks the Soviets were building. In fact, the BTs were only being built at Kharkov; there were at least 30 other tank factories scattered all over the Soviet Union. But we shouldn't leave the BTs without discussing their ultimate development – the T-34. Toward the end of 1937, a new tank based on the BT-7M chassis was designed – the A-20. The "A" stood for "Autostradnyi" or Autobahn tank; like the BTs designed to make high-speed dashes on highways. It had a new turret of rolled sloping armor 25mm thick. Hull armor was increased to 60mm front; 25mm side. It weighed 18 tons, and was powered by a new 500 HP BD-2 V/12 aluminum diesel engine. Design modifications evolved into the A-30, then into T-32, with a new hull shape, having 60mm front and 30mm side armor. A new design, completed in 1939, had heavier armor, an improved transmission, a new 76mm L/30 gun, it weighed 26 tons, it was the T-34. It went into production in June 1940 at the Kirov plant; by June 1941, 1225 T-34s had been produced.

The Soviet Union began developing heavy tanks in 1929 at the Kirov-Zavod factory in Leningrad. From 1933 to 1939, they produced the T-35, which weighed 50 tons, had five turrets, and a ten man crew. It had a 76.2mm gun, a 37mm gun, and five MGs; in 1935, a 45mm gun replaced the 37mm. In 1938, new heavy tanks were designed, the T-100 and the SMK; they weighed 56 and 45 tons respectively. They had two turrets mounted warship style. The upper central turret mounted a 76.2mm gun; the lower front turret a 45mm gun. They had 6 – 7 man crews. They were found to be unsatisfactory in the Finnish campaign. In 1939, Kirov began producing the Kliment Voroshilov KV-1; at that time, the Russians considered it to be the best heavy tank in the world. The KV-1 weighed 46 tons, was armed with the 76.2mm L/30.5 gun, and had a five man crew. It had hull and turret armor 75mm thick. It was powered by the same 500 HP V/12 diesel as the T-34. Its top speed was 22 mph, cross-country 7.5 mph, and cruising 15 mph. Over 600 were built at Kirov before June 1941.

Another tank the Russians built in large numbers was the T-60. It weighed 6.5 tons, had a two man crew, mounted a 20mm automatic cannon and 7.62 MG; it carried 30mm armor, and had a speed of 30mph. The T-60s main virtue was that its chassis and 70 HP gasoline engine could be built in an ordinary auto or truck plant. In late 1941, the T-60 was upgraded to the T-70, which weighed nine tons, mounted a 45mm gun, and had a three man crew.

"STUKAS" vs "SHTURMOVIKS"

Since World War II, many writers have tried to explain the enormous Russian losses suffered in 1941, by saying the Red Army's tanks and aircraft were obsolete and outclassed by the German tanks and aircraft. This is simply not true. The Russian tanks and aircraft were good enough to execute the mission they had been designed to accomplish. The Red Army had been equipped and trained to launch the most massive surprise attack in history. The tanks were designed for a high-speed dash into an almost undefended Western Europe. The Red Air Force was trained and equipped to provide tactical air support to the Red Army – period. They were not trained in air-to-air combat or defensive warfare. The Luftwaffe was supposed to be destroyed on the ground in the opening attack. In fact, in the 1930s, the German, Russian, and Japanese militaries were all trained for offensive, not defensive warfare.

In June 1941, the most numerous Russian frontline aircraft were:

The Polikarpov I-16 Type 17 first appeared in 1938. It was a cute tubby plane that resembled the American Gee Bee Super Sportster, a 1930s Thompson Trophy racer, piloted by Jimmy Doolittle, among others. It had a top speed of 326 mph, was highly maneuverable, and heavily armed. It had two 20mm cannons in the wings and two 7.62mm MGs in the engine cowling. It carried six RS.82 rockets or two VAP-6M or ZAP-6 chemical containers. The Russians were the first in the world to equip their planes with rockets.

The Ilyushin 2 "Shturmovik" was armed with two 37mm anti-tank cannons, two 7.62mm MGs, a DAG 10 grenade launcher, eight RS.82 or RS.132 rockets, a 1321 lb bombload or 200 PTAB anti-tank bombs; it had a top speed of 251 mph. The cockpit, engine, and fuel tanks were armored; it was a flying tank. Before Barbarossa, it had no rear gunner; it was designed to meet no air opposition. After Barbarossa, a rear gunner was added.

The Tupolev SB-2 "Katiuska" was a twin-engined tactical bomber, having a bombload of 2200 lbs; it was armed with four 7.62mm MGs, it had a top speed of 255 mph.

The Ilyushin DB-3F was a heavier twin-engined bomber. It had a top speed of 265 mph, a bombload of 4400 lbs, a range of 2500 miles, it was armed with three 7.62mm MGs. It was succeeded by a version designated IL-4; the bombload was increased to 6000 lbs; the range reduced to 1025 miles.

The most common Russian fighters were the Mikoyan/Gurevich MIG-3 and the LAGG-3; both were comparable to the most common German fighter, the Messerschmitt Bf 109. The MIG-3 had a top speed of 360 mph and was armed with one 12.7mm MG and two 7.62mm MGs. It could carry six 56 lb rockets under the wings. The LAGG-3 had a top speed of 350 mph and was armed with one 20mm motor-mounted cannon and two 12.7mm MGs; it also carried six 56 lb rockets.

In June 1941, the most numerous German frontline aircraft were:

The Messerschmitt Bf 109E (ME-109); Bf stood for Bayerische Flugzeugwerke (Bavarian Aircraft Company). The Bf 109 E had a top speed of 354 mph, and was armed with one 20mm cannon in the nose and two 7.9mm MGs in the wings. For their attacks on Russian airfields, they were fitted with canisters that carried about 90 SD 2 fragmentation bombs. These four pound bomblets had pop-out wings that caused them to spin down to the ground like sycamore seeds. They were very effective against parked aircraft.

The Junkers Ju 87 "Stuka" (Sturzkampfflugzeug) dive bomber. The "Stuka" was Germany's most numerous tactical ground attack aircraft. It was a two-seat, single-engine, inverted gull-wing dive-bomber with a top speed of 255 mph. It could carry up to 4000 lbs of bombs in various combinations (550 lb, 1100 lb, 2200 lb, or one 4000 lb.) It was outfitted with myriad armament suites. One very effective version was a tank-buster, armed with a 37mm Flak 18 cannon under each wing. This type destroyed thousands of Russian tanks.

The Junkers Ju 88 was a twin-engined, multi-purpose aircraft: ground attack, bomber, nightfighter, torpedo bomber, etc. It had a top speed of 280 mph, carried 3300 lbs of bombs, and was armed with four 7.9mm MGs.

The Heinkel III was a heavier twin-engined bomber; it was the most numerous bomber in the Luftwaffe in 1941. It had a top speed of 258 mph, a bombload of 4400 lbs, a range of 760 miles, and was armed with one 20mm cannon and five 7.9mm MGs.

"BLITZKREIG"
vs
"OPERATION IN DEPTH"

In 1941, the German and Russian overall battle plans were similar. Each planned a massive surprise attack that would catch the other side unprepared. The Germans called this Blitzkreig; the Russians called it Operation in Depth. Each planned to destroy the others air force on the ground in the initial attack. Each planned to attack on three massive fronts: North, Central, South. The Russians enjoyed a number of important advantages:

1. They had a much larger war industry base; they could produce tanks, planes, artillery and other war material at a rate impossible to the Germans. In June 1941, they had ten times as many tanks, planes, and artillery pieces as the Germans.

2. They had a much larger manpower pool. Aside from a larger population, they had millions of Osaviakhim reservists. They had millions of Gulag troops who were viewed as expendable cannon fodder by Stalin and the NKVD. They put their women to work; the Germans did not.

3. The Soviets had vast territories to trade for time; the Germans did not.

4. The Russians would be attacking into West European countries with highly developed road systems, ideal for mechanized forces. The Germans would be attacking into a third-world wasteland. The Soviet Union had 850,000 miles of road; only 40,000 were paved. There were no first-class highways. Even today, the territory of the former Soviet Union has fewer miles of paved highway than the state of California.

The German war machine received about half of its petroleum from Rumania's Ploesti oilfields. The other half they made synthetically from coal, in a very expensive and complicated process. The Russians planned to destroy the Ploesti oilfields, refineries, storage facilities, etc. with massive air strikes in the first 24 hours. They planned to capture the Ploesti complex in the first 48 hours.

The basic Russian plan of battle on the Northern Front was for the 3rd, 8th, 10th,11th, and 27th Armies to cut off East Prussia, capture Berlin, and drive into the North German Plain. On the Central Front, the 4th, 5th, 6th, and 26th Armies would take Lublin, Krakow, and Warsaw, and drive to Prague. On the Southern Front, the 12th and 18th Mountain Armies would take the Carpathian Mountains. The 9th Heavy Shock Army, supported by the Black Sea Fleet, would take Ploesti and Bucharest, and drive on into Budapest, Vienna, and Munich. Had Stalin attacked before the middle of June, there is little doubt he would have been successful. It would have been difficult to operate the German war machine without the Ploesti petroleum resources.

The German plan, "Barbarossa", was for Army Group North to take Lithuania, Latvia, and Estonia, and drive on into Leningrad. Army Group Center was to take Minsk and Smolensk, and drive on into Moscow. Army Group South was to take Lvov, Kiev, and Kharkov, and drive on to Stalingrad.

Barbarossa was originally planned for May 15th, but Hitler had had to divert a major portion of his resources to a Balkan campaign that took up most of April and May. The German General Staff believed the Soviet Union could be defeated in eight to ten weeks. Incredibly, they made no logistical preparations beyond five months. When winter arrived, the Wehrmacht had no winter uniforms or cold-weather lubricants. This was one of the reasons Stalin did not believe the Germans planned to attack in the summer of 1941. His intelligence sources assured him the Germans had not been stockpiling winter clothes or lubricants. The Germans had not stockpiled them because they thought the war would be over before they would be needed. The General Staff were so confident of a quick victory, that a major portion of German industry was switched from war production to consumer goods in the autumn of 1941. OKW and OKH even proposed that 60 to 80 divisions be moved back to Germany for the winter.

Despite the odds against winning a protracted war, the Germans might have won another 1940 style Blitzkreig had they not made a few unnecessary mistakes:

1. From the beginning of April to the end of May, Hitler diverted a major segment of his Barbarossa forces to the conquest of Yugoslavia and Greece, culminating in a brilliant, but costly, airborne conquest of Crete. Had he not fought this Balkan campaign, he could have launched Barbarossa on May 15th, which would have given him five more weeks of Russian summer to campaign, which turned out to be critical.

2. They should have prepared logistically for winter warfare. Even if they had captured Leningrad, Moscow, and Stalingrad, they should have been prepared to fight a winter campaign, even if it were only a holding operation until Spring.

3. In 1941, German tanks were being produced at a rate of 1000 to 1500 per year. In the Fall of 1940, Hitler had ordered tank production to be increased to a rate of 800 to 1000 per month, but the Army Ordnance Office had dissuaded him, saying it would cost two billion Reichmarks and involve employment of 100,000 skilled workers. Hitler disastrously agreed to set aside the plan temporarily. Had Hitler insisted on the production increase, it could have made a critical difference in 1941.

4. At the same time, the Army Ordnance Office made another disastrous mistake. Hitler had ordered that all the 37mm guns on the Mark III Panzers be replaced by a long-barreled, high-velocity 50mm L/60 guns. Instead, the Ordnance Office replaced the 37mm guns with short-barreled, low-velocity 50mm L/42 guns, which were totally inadequate as anti-tank weapons. When Hitler found out in February 1941, he was furious and never forgave them. It is easy to see why; it made a critical difference in the summer of 1941. Of the 3200 German tanks that drove into Russia in June 1941, 2068 were Mark IIIs. Of the Mark IIIs, 131 were still armed with 37mm guns, 1893 were equipped with the L/42 short-barreled 50mm gun, and only 40 with the L/60 long-barreled 50mm gun. Guderian later said that had all the Mark IIIs been equipped with the high-velocity L/60 guns, the 1941 summer campaign probably would have succeeded. Combined with the ten-fold increase in tank production Hitler had wanted, it would have made an enormous difference.

The forces the Germans launched against the Russians in June 1941 were approximately equal to those they launched against the British and French in May 1940.

	May 1940	
	Germans	**British/French**
Divisions	122	140
Artillery/Mortars	7700	11,000
Tanks	3200	4000
Aircraft	3600	3700
	June 1941	
	Germans	**Soviets**
Divisions	145	360+
Artillery/Mortars	7700+	100,000+
Tanks	3200	35,000+
Aircraft	3800	25,000+

STATISTICS

"If you kill one man, that is murder; if you kill a million men, that is a statistic."
Joseph Stalin

In 1941, the Red Army had thirty armies, which included over 60 tank divisions; sixteen were "Shock Armies." Shock Armies were "blitzkreig" armies that had been heavily reinforced with additional armor, artillery, and motor transport. Originally, they had been correctly labeled "Invasion Armies", but in the late 1930s their names had been changed to the less threatening "Shock Armies." The other fourteen armies had fewer armored vehicles, artillery, and motor transport.

In June 1941, Stalin had fifteen Shock Armies lined up along the German-Rumanian frontier, they were the 3rd, 4th, 5th, 6th, 8th, 9th, 10th, 11th, 12th, 16th, 18th, 19th, 20th, and 21st; the 23rd was on the Finnish border. Aside from the 9th Heavy Shock Army, each of the other fifteen Shock Armies had approximately 2400 tanks, 700 armored vehicles, 4000 cannons and mortars, and 250,000 men.

The 9th Heavy Shock Army had 20 divisions, including six tank divisions, two air divisions, three motorized divisions, and seven rifle divisions. The 9th was commanded by Colonel-General Malinovsky; there were only eight Colonel-Generals in the Red Army. All other Soviet armies were commanded by Major-Generals or Lieutenant-Generals. The

9th had over 3000 tanks and 1000 armored vehicles. Thus, the sixteen Shock Armies had approximately 39,000 tanks, 12,000 armored vehicles, 64,000 cannons and mortars, and 4,000,000 men. There were also 29 NKVD divisions and 10 to 12 heavy artillery regiments.

In addition, there were five Red Army Airborne Corps deployed in the Soviet/German frontier area. An Airborne Corps had 10,500 men, plus a light tank battalion, an artillery battalion, and an anti-tank battalion. On June 12, 1941, the Red Army created the Directorate of Airborne Troops, with orders to immediately create five additional airborne corps. Standard military doctrine dictates that airborne troops are designed for offensive warfare. So it is interesting to note that in June 1941, Stalin felt the need for a 100% increase in his airborne strength. After June 1941, all the Airborne Corps were broken up and the troops assigned to regular infantry divisions; the Red Army needed defensive, not offensive, troops.

The 1st and 2nd Airborne Corps were targeted on Austria and Czechoslovakia; the 4th and 5th were targeted on Germany. The 9th Heavy Shock Army was concentrated on the Rumanian border, targeted on the Ploesti oilfields approximately 100 kilometers away. The 12th and 18th Mountain Armies were deployed on the Rumanian border, targeted on the Carpathian Mountains.

Aside from the regular Red Army forces, Stalin had two other enormous reserve assets that he employed with reckless abandon in the summer of 1941 – the Osoaviakhim and the Gulag. The Osoaviakhim (Society for the Promotion of Aviation and Chemical Defense) was a para-military organization of over 35 million members – a kind of National Guard. They were trained in all the military skills: infantry, engineers, paratroopers, pilots, and guerilla warfare. Over one million Osoaviakhim had been mobilized and sent to the front before the end of July 1941.

Another of Stalin's enormous hidden assets was the vast Gulag (Glavnoe Upravlenie Lagerei - Chief Administration of Camps.) In 1941, the population of the Gulag was approximately 13 million. In 1941, Stalin sent every man in the Gulag capable of carrying a gun to the front. Due to the shortage of Red Army green uniforms, Gulag troops were sent to the front in their black prison uniforms. In July 1941, the Germans were already encountering whole 50,000 man corps of black clad Gulag troops. This meant that Stalin had already mobilized the Gulag army before the Germans attacked. Obviously, they had been dragooned into service to support Stalin's planned July offensive. Their numbers and impact on the fighting were enormous. Reportedly, Rokossovsky's army was made up almost entirely of Gulag troops. They were considered to be expendable. Backed by NKVD retreat-blocking troops, they were often the first wave in an attack. The Red Army didn't bother using combat engineers to clear German minefields in an assault. When the British offered mine detectors to General Ratov, the head of the Soviet Military Mission in Britain, the General declined, explaining that "in the Soviet Union we use people." Marshal Zhukov told General Eisenhower that he used Gulag troops to clear minefields with their feet. With NKVD troops pointing machine guns at their backs, Gulag troops cleared the minefields by charging through them.

With such vast unlimited expendable reserves, it is no wonder the Germans became discouraged and demoralized. No matter how many Russians they killed or captured, they always found themselves facing a horde of fresh troops. By 1941, Stalin had already murdered tens of millions of innocent people pursuing his internal agenda of control; so losing tens of millions more in defense of the Motherland was, as he would put it - "statistical."

A MASTERPIECE

"The enemy must be caught unawares, and the time chosen when his troops are scattered."
Stalin (Vol. 6, p.158)

In November 1938, Trotsky wrote: "Stalin finally untied Hitler's hands, as well as those of his enemies, and thereby pushed Europe towards war." On June 21, 1939, Trotsky said: "The Soviet Union will move up to the German frontiers in all its massed strength just at the moment when the Third Reich becomes involved in the conflict for a new repartition of the world." On the same day, Trotsky also prophesied that Poland would be occupied in the autumn and that Germany would attack the Soviet Union in the autumn of 1941.

Hitler and Stalin had agreed to attack Poland simultaneously in September 1939. Had they done so, Britain and France would have had to declare war on Germany and the Soviet Union in order to fulfill their agreement with Poland to come to their aid if attacked. Such a monumental undertaking would have been unthinkable to Britain and France. At the last minute Stalin pleaded that his forces would not be ready by September 1st, but for Hitler to go ahead as scheduled and the Red Army would launch its supporting attack in two weeks. The British and French felt emboldened to take on the Germans alone. Thus, Stalin faked Hitler into attacking alone, and getting the blame for starting World War II.

In his *MEMOIRS*, Nikita Khrushchev reported that Stalin was exultant after the Molotov-Ribbentrop Pact was signed on August 23, 1939. "I have deceived him. I have deceived Hitler," Stalin cried joyfully. Hitler had been maneuvered into starting a new European war only a week and a half after the Pact had been signed. It was the case of a casino crapshooter versus a chess grandmaster.

Hitler went ahead on his own thinking Britain and France would back down at the last minute as they had in the case of Czechoslovakia in 1938. Also, Hitler didn't believe Britain and France would be crazy enough to start World War II over Poland. Especially since, he reasoned, they had no way to come to Poland's aid in any case. Stalin had always been a chess master. Before the Revolution, he had regularly beaten Lenin and Trotsky, who were supposed to be good. Thus, Stalin got his long planned European war started and got his stooge Hitler to get blamed for executing Stalin's plan. A Stalinist masterpiece!

As previously stated, Stalin's original plan was to get Hitler to start the war, then launch the Red Army into Europe after the British, French, and Germans had bled themselves white in a stalemated slaughterhouse. When the Germans "blitzed" the British and French in six weeks in May-June 1940, Stalin had to revise his plan. Stalin now decided to wait until the German forces were completely occupied with conquering Britain (Operation Sealion) to launch his assault. Stalin calculated that the German forces would be fighting in Britain and clinging like crabs to the coastline of France and Belgium.

At that moment, Stalin would launch his 300 divisions, 35,000 tanks, 30,000 aircraft, and 55,000 paratroopers to sweep into a practically undefended Western Europe. The Rumanian Ploesti oilfields would be taken in the first 48 hours in a massive armored and airborne assault. In a stroke, the German war machine would have no fuel to run on. When the tens of thousands of high-speed BT-7s, A-20s, and T-60s reached the Reich's vast Autobahn network, Germany itself would be overrun in a matter of days.

The Red Army would be setting on the Rhine and occupying the Ruhr industrial heartland. The Germans would have to immediately disengage from Operation Sealion, and send their armed forces dashing pell-mell for the Fatherland. About the best they could hope for would be to meet the Red Army at the Rhine, with the Russians in control of their industry, their petroleum, and das Volk. It appeared to be a perfect plan.

Before the ink was dry on the Molotov-Ribbentrop Nonaggression Pact of August 23, 1939, Stalin violated the terms of the territorial divisions that had been agreed upon. First he invaded Finland (November 1939 to March 1940); next he seized the Baltic states (June to August 1940); at the same time he threatened and intimidated the Rumanian government into letting him send the Red Army into the provinces of Bessarabia and Bukovina (June 1940), putting it 100 kilometers from the Ploesti oilfields. These moves were accompanied by massive reinforcements of Russia's western frontier zone by the Red Army. This was at a time when German forces were massed on the coast of France, preparing to invade Britain. Germany's increasing vulnerability was obvious. Ribbentrop recalled that beginning in July 1940, Hitler became increasingly worried about these Soviet activities.

Joachim von Ribbentrop, *THE RIBBENTROP MEMOIRS,* Weiderfeld and Nicolson, London, 1954), p.146.

According to Dr. Paul Otto Schmidt, Ribbentrop's aide and personal translator, Hitler decided to make one final attempt to reach some *modus vivendi* with the Soviet Union during meetings in Berlin on November 12-13, 1940. These meetings between Hitler (with Foreign Minister Ribbentrop)

and Molotov (with Ambassador Dekanosov) were intended
by Hitler to reach a preliminary agreement on nothing less
than the division of the world among Germany, Russia, Japan,
and Italy. Hitler tried to direct Russia's interest southward to
the Middle East and India. Hitler calculated that this would
fulfill Russia's historic dream "to wash the dusty boots of our
soldiers in the warm waters of the Indian Ocean." Molotov
was interested, but stubbornly pressed their claims in Europe
and the Baltic. Discussions between Hitler and Molotov
became heated and ill-tempered. The meeting ended with
Hitler concluding that it would be impossible to reach any
long-term accommodation with the Russians.

Dr. Paul (Otto) Schmidt, *HITLER'S INTERPRETER*,
Macmillan Co, NYC, 1951, pp. 209-220.

"(B)y their aggressive actions, Stalin and Molotov
by mid-1940 had profoundly alarmed and infuriated
Hitler. At that time Moscow had begun making brazen
demands on the Germans, such as insisting on giving
the USSR a unilateral free hand in the oil-rich Middle
East, the Balkans, Finland, and the Turkish Straits, while
threatening to seize the Rumanian oil fields."
Weeks, op. cit., p. 137.

At the meetings, Stalin (via Molotov) had demanded
control of Finland, the Baltic, the Balkans (Bulgaria, Hungary,
Rumania, Yugoslavia), Greece, the Dardanelles, and the
Middle East. The Baltic would have become a Russian lake,
with the Red Fleet threatening the transport of Swedish iron
ore to Germany. The Red Army was already poised only
100 kilometers from the Ploesti oilfields – Hitler's jugular.
Germany would have been encircled from the Baltic to the
Balkans. Defense against a Soviet attack would have been
impossible; Germany would have become a Soviet satellite.

In 1939, Germany imported 45% of its iron ore, 25% of its zinc, 50% of its lead, 70% of its copper, 90% of its tin, 95% of its nickel, 99% of its bauxite, 66% of its mineral oils, and 80% of its rubber. (Topitsch, op. cit., p.46.) These basic elements came from or through the Soviet Union. Thus, up until June 1941, Stalin controlled most of the raw materials that the German war machine ran on.

While the Soviets shipped raw materials to the Germans, they demanded armaments and industrial equipment in return. This enabled them to evaluate German armaments technology and industrial capacity, which reinforced their feeling of superiority. Stalin knew the Soviet armaments industry and war machine enjoyed overwhelming supremacy. Thus, he felt completely confident to make his crushing demands in November 1940. Molotov's rude and excessive demands amounted to an ultimatum. They alarmed and enraged Hitler and set in motion his preparations to attack Stalin.

In seizing Bessarabia and Bukovina, Stalin made one of the few mistakes of his career. The German war machine ran on Rumanian oil. The Ploesti oilfields were the first target of Stalin's planned conquest of Europe. Seeing the Germans totally absorbed in their "blitzkreig", Stalin had gotten eager and tipped his hand. From that moment, Hitler could not take his eyes off the Red Army poised 100 kilometers from his jugular. This and the heroic stand of the RAF, prompted him to turn his gaze eastward and begin to plan "Operation Barbarossa."

Seeing Hitler abandon "Operation Sealion" and begin to move his forces eastward, Stalin again had to revise his plans. Stalin now planned to launch a giant surprise attack before Hitler could get his forces positioned along the Polish/Rumanian frontier. Stalin planned to launch his attack on Sunday, July 6, 1941. Like the Japanese, Stalin and Zhukov liked surprise attacks on Sunday mornings. Though Stalin's original plan of attacking either a helpless and exhausted

Europe or a fully engaged Germany would have been better, he still had every reason to believe he would be successful. Stalin knew that he had at his disposal war material an order of magnitude greater than Hitler's. The Red Army had more than ten times as many tanks and guns as the Wehrmacht. The Red Air Force had over ten times as many planes as the Luftwaffe. And his powerful forces were poised 100 kilometers from the lifeblood of Hitler's war machine – Ploesti. After the first 48 hours, Hitler's war machine would have no fuel to operate on. Stalin was optimistic.

Hitler was also optimistic. He had just destroyed in six weeks French and British forces that had more divisions, more artillery, and in the case of the French, more and better tanks. In fact, for some reason, the French Army was rated the best in the world. Most important of all, he believed Stalin's war machine was a house of cards. As Hitler put it: "You have only to kick in the door, and the whole rotten structure will come crashing down." He had valid reasons for believing this. In the winter of 1940, the tiny Finnish Army had made monkeys of the vaunted Red Army. The Red Army needed over one and a half million men and three months to bring off an operation that should have taken two to three weeks. Khrushchev said the Red Army lost almost one million men in the Finnish campaign. This confirmed the general belief that Stalin had ripped the heart out of the Red Army in the Purges of 1937 – 1938. During the Purges, Stalin killed more officers above the rank of Colonel than were killed by the Germans during the war.

In the 1930s, Stalin had learned that you can kill millions of people and a society will continue to function, if your apparatus of compulsion is strong and ruthless enough. Thus, he knew decimating the command element would not kill the Red Army.

PREEMPTION

Any one of Stalin's plans would have worked. The French and British should have been able to stop the Germans; they had more tanks and airplanes. The French had the "magnificent" French Army "the best in the world" plus the "invincible" Maginot Line. The French Somua S-35 and Char-B were a match for the German Mark III and Mark IV. The Somua S-35 had 55mm of armor, the Char-B had 60mm; the Mark III and Mark IV had 30mm of armor. Their guns were about equal, but German anti-tank projectiles bounced harmlessly off the Char-B. Generally, German fighters and tactical aircraft were better than their French or British counterparts; but the British Spitfire was better than the Messerschmitt Me-109.

The Germans concentrated their tank divisions in Panzer Corps; the French spread their tanks out through the army as infantry support. The French set the 9th Army under General Corap to guard the "impenetrable" Ardennes. The 9th Army was made up of old poorly armed and trained reservists and fortress troops. On May 10, 1940, the Germans sent seven Panzer divisions charging through the Ardennes and the 9th Army; on June 25th, the French surrendered. The bloody World War I style stalemate Stalin had envisioned did not take place.

As previously recounted, in June 1940, while the Wehrmacht was busy "blitzing" France, Stalin seized the

Rumanian province of Bessarabia. This put the Red Army 100 kilometers from Ploesti; 100 kilometers from Hitler's jugular. It tipped Stalin's hand. It alerted Hitler to Stalin's plan. From that moment Hitler had one eye on Britain and one eye on Stalin. Hitler knew he had to attack Stalin before Stalin attacked him.

After the six week "blitzkreig" in France, Stalin and the world thought the British would be "a piece of cake." As the world knows, the Brits fought like wildcats. The RAF beat the "invincible" Luftwaffe. Hitler realized "the game was not worth the candle." Hitler also realized that his real war was against Stalin, and if it were to be done "'twere well it were done quickly."

Everyone, including Hitler and Stalin, knew that the biggest mistake Germany made in World War I was fighting a war on two fronts. At a meeting with the High Command on 11/23/39, Hitler stated that war with the Soviet Union could only begin after the war in the West was finished. Stalin knew war on two fronts would be crazy and suicidal for Hitler; he was certain Hitler was not crazy or suicidal.

Stalin saw the Luftwaffe's brilliant airborne assault on Crete in May 1941 as a dress rehearsal for the coming invasion of Britain. He was patiently waiting for Operation Sealion to get well underway before launching his own war. Soviet intelligence assured him the Germans were not preparing to attack Russia. General Golikov of the GRU had an army of agents in Europe monitoring industries such as the sheep and petroleum industries. If Hitler were planning to invade the Soviet Union, he would need millions of sheepskin coats. The clothing industry would have to start producing millions of sheepskin coats. Millions of sheep would have to be slaughtered leading to a fall in mutton prices and a rise in sheepskin prices. This did not happen because the Wehrmacht did not order millions of sheepskin coats.

If Hitler were planning to invade the Soviet Union, he would need winter lubricants that would not congeal making engine and weapon parts freeze together. He would need fuel that would not break down in severe cold and become incombustible. The Wehrmacht did not procure winter fuels and lubricants. The GRU assured Stalin the Wehrmacht was not stockpiling millions of sheepskin coats or winter grade fuels and lubricants. They could not be preparing to invade the Soviet Union.

Hitler launched Operation Barbarossa without preparing for winter warfare in Russia. The usual explanation is that the General Staff believed the Red Army would be defeated in eight to ten weeks, which is the way it looked in the beginning. It is also possible that German intelligence was aware GRU was monitoring preparations for winter warfare and decided not to tip their hand. The fact is, Hitler had no idea of the vast resources in equipment, manpower, and productive capacity Stalin had at his disposal.

In June 1941, Hitler and Stalin each dreamed of soon reigning supreme over a vast Eurasian Empire stretching from the Atlantic to the Pacific. These pagan gods would rule a millennial world populated with either "Aryan Supermen" or "New Socialist Men." It was the heady stuff of ancient totalitarian dreams.

It is no wonder Stalin reportedly went into shock and disappeared for days, when Hitler launched his surprise preemptive attack on June 22, 1941. The Red Army was caught poised in forward offensive positions, ready to launch their surprise attack in July 1941. Hitler had Stalin for breakfast, before Stalin had Hitler for lunch. Over twenty years of frantic and ruthless preparation were suddenly obliterated. The Five-Year Plans, the Collectivization, the Famines, the Show Trials, the Purges, the Gulag; all in preparation for his triumphal conquests, were shattered in an instant.

Had Stalin attacked before Hitler, the world would have witnessed a lightning war that would have made Hitler's 1940 "blitzkreig" in France look like a Girl Scout Jamboree. Tens of thousands of airborne troops would have blanketed strategic targets in Rumania, Poland, and Germany. Over 100,000 Russian cannons would have obliterated German positions at the breakthrough points. Tens of thousands of Red Air Force planes would have blasted airfields and key targets. Tens of thousands of Red Army high speed tanks would have swept into Germany, Austria, Hungary, Rumania, and Czechoslovakia. In their wake would have poured hundreds of thousands of NKVD troops. Millions of West European political leaders, officer corps, all of academe and the intelligentsia would have been slaughtered. The NKVD would have attempted to obliterate all potential future leaders. There would have been thousands of "Katyn Forests" massacres all over Europe. This would have been the introductory "pacification" stage. Then the shipments of millions to the Gulag would have commenced. This was Stalin's plan. This is what he had done to his own people in the 1930s. The Mongol conquests would have looked like an "ice cream social."

"On 5 March 1940 the Politburo resolved to shoot 25,700 former Polish officers, clerks, landowners, industrialists, gendarmes, and other members of the Polish elite in prisoner-of-war camps in the Ukraine and Belorussia. In April-May 1940 a total of 21,857 people were shot. Stalin obviously was trying to thwart any potential attempts to restore the prewar Polish state."

Oleg V. Khlevniuk, *The History of the Gulag, From Collectivization to the Great Terror*, Yale University Press, New Haven & London, 2004, p.237.

BACKGROUND

"Communism is the greatest man-made disaster in history....
It's central concept, the state ownership of human beings,
has no place anywhere."
Ken Adelman

This section of the book tries to show what would have
happened to the people of Europe in the 1940s and beyond
had Stalin been able to impose his monstrous system on them.
It tries to explain the fundamental nature of the system Lenin
and Stalin created, and to describe the incredible suffering
and slaughter it caused. Some post-World War II history of
the CPSU and the KGB are covered; but primary attention is
focused on the activities of the CPSU and the NKVD during
the 1930s. Attention is also focused on the vast Gulag and the
tens of millions of innocent people who perished in this frozen
hell.

Since World War II, most writers have concentrated on the
numbers of people exterminated by the Nazis; until recently,
very few people seemed to be aware that the Communists had
slaughtered a vastly larger number. Writers on Communist
exterminations dealt almost exclusively with the millions who
died in the Collectivizations and the Purges; their estimates
of the numbers who had died in the Gulag system always appeared to be entirely too low.

Inasmuch as there were literally decades during which tens of millions of people passed through the Gulag system, and all reports of escapees spoke of appalling death rates, it became obvious that the numbers who died in the Gulag, had to be much larger than the combined totals of those who died from other causes. In support of this hypothesis, data were compiled on estimated Gulag populations and death rates in various periods. These data were combined with the estimated death tolls from other causes, such as the Purges and Collectivization, to arrive at an overall total extermination figure chargeable to the Communist Party of the Soviet Union (CPSU). The total figure arrived at was approximately 107,000,000; the Soviet Union had been a vast slaughterhouse - an abattoir.

On page 10 of *GULAG ARCHIPELAGO*, Aleksandr Solzenitsyn estimated that ..."internal repression cost us, from the beginning of the October Revolution up to 1959, a total of...sixty-six million - 66,000,000 - lives." Note "up to 1959."

In *LETHAL POLITICS*, R. J. Rummel estimated that between 28,326,000 and 126,891,000 people were killed by the CPSU between 1917 and 1987; calling 61,911,000 a most prudent estimate. Most evidence now suggests the 126,891,000 estimate is closer to the truth.

In recent years, a group of Russian intellectuals calling itself The Memorial Association, published data released from the central archives in Moscow blaming the Stalin regime for 84 million deaths: "19 million killed during the purges, 22 million killed during forced collectivization, 34 million killed during World War 11, 6 to 9 million killed between the end of the war and Stalin's death in 1953." Again note "in 1953."

Roman Krutsyk of Kiev Memorial has stated that newly discovered documents reveal that between 1917 and 1991, the Bolshevik regime killed approximately "50 million ethnic Ukrainians within the borders of the Soviet Union."

Jeffrey Kuhner, Opportunity in Ukraine, *The Washington Times*, 10/21/03.

Roman Krutsyk estimates that during this 1917-1991 period, the Bolshevik regime killed approximately 130,000,000 people overall.
E-mails from: "UCCA"<*ucca@i.kiev.ua*> dated 1and 4 April 2005.

Memorial prints lists of the dead in books the size of telephone directories. The Memorial group calls the Stalin regime the moral equivalent of the Hitler regime. It is also trying to organize an international tribunal that would put the Stalin regime on trial in the same way that the Hitler regime was tried at Nuremberg in 1946. Millions who committed the horrible acts of betrayal, torture, and murder described herein remain unpunished.

The Soviet economy was a slave economy. The Soviet Union was always short of conventional capital on the world market. They never had the enormous amounts of capital needed for the gigantic industrial projects they implemented. Tens of millions of slaves became their capital.

The slaves of the ante-bellum South were expensive to obtain and needed to be preserved to extract their maximum value over a lifetime. The slaves of the Soviet Union cost the State nothing and the supply was inexhaustible. So the logical thing to do was to extract the maximum value as quickly as possible at the lowest possible cost. This is how the Soviet economy "worked" from 1917 to 1992.

The only industry the Soviet Union ever successfully developed was the world's largest armaments industry. This was the only industry the Party ever had any interest in developing. A consumer industry was developed only to the extent required to provide the citizens with the minimum basic necessities of food, clothing, and shelter. The "free" citizenry were maintained at a level only marginally better than the confined citizenry of the Gulag. Thus, the average "comrade" cost the Party little more to maintain than the average "zek" in the Gulag.

Probably over ninety percent of the prisoners in the Gulag were political prisoners who were innocent of any crime. "Politicals" were the ones who were tortured in Sukhanovka and subjected to the cruelest abuse in the Gulag. Murderers and thieves were not considered a threat to the Party's control, therefore, in the Gulag they were the trustees and informers who assisted the NKVD in controlling the "politicals."

It should also be kept in mind that probably ninety percent of the political prisoners were innocent of any resistance to the Party's control. They were arrested by the tens of millions for two reasons. First, the Party could maintain absolute control only by inducing unremitting abject fear in the masses. Second, the Soviet economy was based on slave labor. It could not have survived without this vast pool of unpaid labor who could be forced to perform all the dangerous and difficult projects needed by the State. The Soviet system never worked; only terror and slave labor kept it alive for 75 years.

Several fundamental facts need to be clearly established in order to comprehend the magnitude of the Gulag nightmare. First, the physical facilities of even the Nazi death camps like Auschwitz and Treblinka were five-star luxury accommodations compared to the best camps in the Gulag. Second, bookkeeping in all Soviet industrial enterprises from 1917 to 1991 was totally corrupt and bore no resemblance to reality. This was true of all industry: the steel industry, the clothing industry, or the Gulag industry. The administrator had to meet the Gosplan quotas, or the administrator was shot or shipped to the Gulag. Thus, all books in all Soviet enterprises were "cooked." If all archives were thrown open tomorrow, Gulag accounting would make Enron's books look like the model of fiduciary responsibility. All production and death rates were "tweaked" to meet the quotas.

THE TERROR MACHINE

"Russia is a nation occupied by an internal enemy."
Eugene Lyons, *WORKERS PARADISE LOST*, p.54.

"There is a simple word which explains most things in
Russia ...It is 'fear'. It is almost impossible for people in
Western countries to understand how constant, universal
and ever present is the element of fear among people of
the Soviet Union."
V. and E. Petrov, *EMPIRE OF FEAR*, p. 75.

For 75 years The Communist Party of the Soviet Union
(CPSU) succeeded in duping the "liberal" element of Western
"intelligentsia" (whom Lenin and Stalin called "poleznye
idioty"– useful idiots) into eagerly believing the CPSU were
creating a Utopia – a perfect, classless, egalitarian society – a
"Worker's Paradise." Let us "pierce the veil" of the "Worker's
Paradise" and examine the fundamental nature of the CPSU
and its Janis-like control apparatus – the NKVD/KGB.

Analysts have occupied themselves with the tip of the
iceberg, by studying such superficial manifestations and
characteristics as ideology, tactical shifts, economic reforms,
reorganizations etc., which are interesting, but essentially irrelevant. More effort should have been devoted to analyzing
the Communist system from the standpoint of its being the

most efficient political and social surveillance and control
mechanism ever developed. It was designed to enable a small
group of men to exercise total control of every form of activity
within their domain. Stalin and Bukharin were not indulging
in hyperbole when they said:

"…the world has never known such a mighty party
as our Communist party."
I. V. Stalin, *WORKS, XIII*, p. 231.

(The Communist Party) "is a gigantic machine, the
like of which mankind has not seen in any era of its existence."
N.I. Bukharin, *IZVESTIA*, 3/30/34.

These were not exaggerations; the Party elite, the "nomenklatura", and their full-time professional Party personnel, the
"apparatchiks", over the years established the most thorough
and comprehensive cross-check surveillance and control apparatus ever created. The Communist system was in essence
a police mechanism; any of its other characteristics were
incidental to this fundamental fact. Let us commence our
assessment of this police system masquerading as a socio/
economic movement, by running through its incredibly comprehensive surveillance and control structure.

In the mid-1930s, the NKVD had a full-time strength of
over two million full-time agents, supplemented by a vast
ancillary network. There were the "stukachi", a part-time
informer network, numbering twenty million; the People's
Squads, numbering about six million; the Brigades for
Assisting the Militia; street committees; apartment wardens;
etc.

Robert Conquest, *THE SOVIET SECRET POLICE SYSTEM*, pp. 62-68.

The CPSU had a PPO or cell, operating in every economic, military, or social organization in the Soviet Union; keeping under full-time surveillance everything that went on in every factory, farm, school, barracks, ship, sports club, etc. One of the Party's key surveillance and control appendages was the Komsomol, the All-Union Leninist Young Communist League. The Komsomol was the CPSU's youth auxiliary, it was the Party's chief source of new members, and its primary propaganda instrument among the young.

It was composed of persons between fourteen and twenty-eight, and numbered approximately twenty million. Founded in 1918, the Konsomol was largely responsible for the Bolshevik's victory in the Civil War, and the Party's success in establishing their system. They were the Party's chief source of revolutionary activists, and provided both troops and commanders for the Red Army.

The Party thoroughly exploited all the usual revolutionary characteristics of youth: fanaticism, boldness, thirst for adventure, naive idealism, and nosy meddlesomeness. The Konsomol was one of the Party's prime movers in implementing all their massive programs such as collectivization and the five-year plans. Their activities had much in common with that of the Red Guards later in China. The Party apparatus used the mass membership of the CPSU and the Konsomol as "front" organizations, just as it manipulated "useful idiot" groups like the Western media and academe to achieve its objectives.

The final control mechanism was the military establishment, the most powerful military force in the world. This was the major repository of physical force at the disposal of the Party; however, it also constituted the greatest potential threat to its position, and as such, had to be kept under constant surveillance and supervision. Therefore, at every level from platoon up, the Party apparatus had political personnel, "Zampolits", working side by side with their military counterpart, supervising their every move. In addition, the NKVD had their own "Special Section" personnel, operating at all levels, and supplemented with a vast secret informer network. This NKVD network watched both the military and political personnel.

The NKVD and the political personnel were part of structures that were parallel but separate from the military structure. At every level they outranked their military counterpart in final authority and reported up through their own chain of command. This arrangement kept the military on the verge of psychosis. The military and the NKVD had the necessary organization and power to seize control of the country at any time. To counter such a threat, the Party apparatus kept them under full-time intensive surveillance, to prevent any kind of conspiracy from getting started. To finalize his total control, Stalin had to completely subjugate the Red Army and the NKVD. During the Great Purges, he had the NKVD murder the command structure and terrorize the Red Army. He then had the command structure of the NKVD murdered.

An omnipresent atmosphere of fear and suspicion permeated every component of life in the Soviet Union. To try to understand how the creation of such an all-powerful totalitarian apparatus was possible, we need to go back to the days of the Mongol conquest. To begin with, Russia lived under Mongol/Tartar rule for 200 years, from 1238 to 1452; during this period, the Oriental concept of centralized-absolutist government was firmly established. It is also worth remembering that one of the principal reasons the Mongols were so incredibly successful at conquest, was that they utilized unlimited terror, cruelty, and extermination against all who opposed them. The Mongol "hordes" had a tremendous impact on Eastern and Western civilization, but on no one as much as the people of the area that is now the Soviet Union. It is not without reason that there exists an old proverb: "Scratch a Russian and you will find a Tartar."

This totalitarian tradition was continued by the Tsars for the next 450 years; during this time, many of the seeds of Communist Party system were implanted:
* there was very little freedom of speech or press;
* there was police registration and internal passports;
* the secret police organization was established;
* there was no legal procedure for redressing grievances against the government;
* travel abroad was discouraged or prevented; foreigners were viewed with suspicion;
* the State religion, orthodoxy, was basically a communal religion, emphasizing congregational salvation, rather than individual. It also emphasized conformity; any form of deviation was a sin;
* the majority of the farmers were organized in communal structures called Mirs. Nineteenth century Russian intellectuals glorified the Mirs as the ideal social structure of the future. General acceptance of the concept of the Mir by the peasantry, who constituted 90 percent of the population, greatly facilitated the widespread acceptance of the Communist Party's other ideas of communal organization of society.
Herbert McClosky and John E. Turner, *THE SOVIET DICTATORSHIP*, pp.21-30.

In order to better understand the structure and methodology of the Communist system of control as it evolved, it is necessary to extract the essence of Leninism, and to examine the philosophy of a man who greatly influenced the formation of its basic character – Sergei G. Nechaev. Sergei Nechaev (1847-1883) was a Russian revolutionary leader, who is credited with being one of the principal founders of modern terrorism. He despised the human race and all its institutions, and was the author of some of the wildest plans for total destruction ever written. Dostoyesky used him as the model for Peter Verkhovensky in *THE DEVILS*, and he and his disciples as the models for his revolutionaries in *THE POSSESSED*.

Nechaev demanded that the revolutionary exorcise from his being every vestige of humanity, compassion, and love, and be ready to deceive, exploit, torture, and murder any required number of people, including one's family and best friends, for the sake of the cause. He recommended killing everyone over age 25. Nechaev believed that the masses were only needed to help overthrow the existing order; that they must be led by a revolutionary elite; that they must recognize the foresight and wisdom of this elite, and therefore be willing to follow and obey.

Lenin used Nechaev's organizational structure, with its small Central Committee as a model for the Bolshevik organization. Trotsky in *OUR POLITICAL TASKS* said:

"Lenin's organization is calculated for a party which puts itself in the place of the working class and acts in their name and for them, without taking any notice of what the workers feel and think."

In 1869 while Nechaev was living in Geneva with Mikhail Bakunin, a pioneer anarchist, the two collaborated in writing probably the most extremist revolutionary document of all time, the *CATECHISM OF THE REVOLUTIONARY*. Several illustrative articles of the Catechism were extracted from Robert Payne's *ZERO* and Franco Venture's *ROOTS OF REVOLUTION:*

#1. "The revolutionary is a lost man; he has no interests of his own, no cause of his own, no feelings, no habits, no belongings;…. Everything in him is absorbed by a single, exclusive interest, a single thought, a single passion – the revolution.

#2. In the very depths of his being ... he has broken every tie with the civil order, with...all laws, conventions and... ethics of this world. He will be an implacable enemy of this world, and if he continues to live in it, that will only be so as to destroy it the more effectively.

#3. The revolutionary ... knows only one science, that of destruction.

#4. He despises ... the existing social ethic...; for him, everything that allows the triumph of the revolution is moral, and everything that stands in its way is immoral.

#6. All the tender feelings of family life, of friendship, love, gratitude and even honour must be stifled.... For him there is only one pleasure,...the success of the revolution. Day and night he must have one single thought,...merciless destruction. With this aim in view, tirelessly and in cold blood, he must always be prepared to die and to kill with his own hands anyone who stands in the way of achieving it.

#13. The revolutionary... lives in this world only because he has faith in its quick and complete destruction. He should not hesitate to destroy any position, any place, or any man in this world. He must hate everyone and everything with an equal hatred. All the worse for him if he has in the world relationships with parents, friends, or lovers; he is no longer a revolutionary if he is swayed by these relationships."

Lenin's definition of a revolutionary is almost pure Nechaev:

"...the revolutionary is not a revolutionary if he has any sympathy for this world. He should not hesitate to destroy any position, any place or any man in this world. He must hate every one and everything in it with equal hatred. All the worse for him if he has any relations with

parents, friends or lovers; he is no longer a revolutionary
if he is swayed by these relationships."

The influence of Nechaev is also reflected in Lenin's
views on morality:

"In what sense do we repudiate ethics and morality?
In the sense that they were preached by the bourgeoisie,
who declared that ethics were God's commandments.
We, of course, say that we do not believe in God....
We say: Morality is that which serves to destroy the
old exploiting society and to unite all toilers around the
proletariat, which is creating a new Communist society.
Communist morality is the morality which serves this
struggle...."

V. I. Lenin, "The Tasks of the Youth League", Oct.
2, 1920.

With conscience and morality given a completely twisted
meaning, and with fair-play and compassion dispensed
with, fear remained the only available control device. Julius
Martov, a co-founder with Lenin of *ISKRA (THE SPARK)*,
and later the founder of the Menshevik movement, not only
accused Lenin of using Marxism as a facade, but denounced
Lenin as a Nechaevist.

Alexander Gambarov in his *THE DISPUTE OVER
NECHAEV*, said that the Bolsheviks used Nechaev as their
model.

"Nechaevism became a symbol for everything con-
nected with falsehood, deceit, the criminal, fantastic and
uncontrolled arbitrariness of a central institution lacking
any supervision, and intent on snaring unsuspecting ide-
alists."

Michael Prowdin, *THE UNMENTIONABLE
NECHAEV*, p.107.

"Lenin had little interest in Marxism as a scientific theory." He argued instead…"that the party would owe its strength not to its ideological superiority or the size of its membership but to its degree of organization."

Abdurakhman Avtorkhanov, *THE COMMUNIST PARTY APPARATUS*, pp.2,9.

Stalin himself defined the essence of Leninism thusly: "The basic question of Leninism, its starting point, is … the question of the dictatorship of the proletariat, of the conditions of its conquest and the conditions of its consolidation."

I. V. Stalin, *PROBLEMS OF LENINISM*, p. 35.

Some of Lenin's contemporaries came to realize he was willing to do or promise anything in order to seize power; any philosophy and program of government was incidental to this objective. As Eugene Lyons put it: "Beyond a determination to capture the revolution and a Machiavellian code of conduct, the Bolsheviks…had no plan."

Eugene Lyons, *WORKERS PARADISE LOST*, p. 38.

In the pre-putsch days, *PRAVDA (TRUTH)*, then edited by Stalin and Molotov, promised the people that a Bolshevik victory would bring freedom, justice, fair labor laws, the right of non-Russian nationalities to establish independent nations; in short, everything they knew the people wanted. The ideology, the slogans, and the utopian goals were only a facade, a necessary device for deceiving the masses. The Bolshevik leadership always realized that in order to justify the terrible sacrifices and repressions, they had to promise it was leading to the millennium. Lenin used the ideology of Marx primarily as a convenient garment in which to camouflage his new totalitarian organization of society. Ideology became, and remained, little more than a "card index" of useful quotations from which the Party leaders selected a slogan applicable to the tactics of the moment.

According to Marx, capitalism represented repression of the workers by the bourgeoisie; socialism was to represent repression of the bourgeoisie by the workers. Marx called for a "dictatorship of the proletariat", by which he meant self-government by the workers. Lenin developed the concept of a dictatorship of the Party apparatus, and substituted it for Marx's "dictatorship of the proletariat"; calling the CPSU apparatus the "vanguard of the proletariat". Thus, Lenin betrayed the basic mission of Marxism and the socialist movement by freeing the workers from the chains of one set of masters, and locking them in the iron grip of another. Marxism is socialist ideology; Leninism is a system of control.

Lenin's own definition of the CPSU dictatorship was:

> "A scientific interpretation of dictatorship means nothing else but a government unlimited by any laws, and absolutely unhampered by any rules and relying directly on force."
> V. I. Lenin, *WORKS, XXV*, p. 441.

Lenin viewed all states as dictatorships, calling them: "special apparatuses for compulsion". Lenin was the architect of the absolute police state. This was his contribution to the principles of Marxism-Leninism; he was the designer of the control mechanism.

The elite of the Party proclaimed themselves the "vanguard of the proletariat", self-appointed to rule in their name; a tidy form of electioneering, but one that requires very efficient machinery of compulsion to make it stick. It therefore became necessary to establish a vast surveillance and control network that would enable them to watch and manipulate everything, and be willing to use this machinery to torture, imprison, or exterminate as many people as required to thwart the development of any opposition. Comrade Stalin was probably the first member of the ruling elite to fully appreciate the true potential of this machine. He correctly perceived that here was the means to permanently enslave the masses. Lenin invented the machine; Stalin perfected it; and *1984* arrived 50 years early – in the 1930s.

In the process of guarding its own position and an outdated ideology, the Party became, in essence, a police organization; fundamentally identical to the NKVD. The NKVD were often referred to as the "Terror Machine," and yet they and the Party performed the identical function of surveillance and control, with the identical mission of keeping themselves in power. Thus, for all practical purposes, they were identical. The CPSU and the NKVD were the "Terror Machine."

"There are ... those who believe, that the term 'Soviet law' is a contradiction in terms. The widespread use of terror as an administrative tool in the Soviet Union justifies this belief. The Polish philosopher, Leszik Kolakowski, has written that Lenin laid the foundations for the system of law characteristic of totalitarianism, as opposed to the laws of a despotic system."

"In despotism, the characteristic feature is the severity of the law. What is characteristic of a totalitarian system is the law's fictitious nature. In reality, the law does not exist, nor for that matter does the penal code. A rule of law cannot exist when the KGB secret police decides what the law and the penal code are."

Arnold Beichman, "Could this bear sell you the Brooklyn Bridge?", The Washington Times, 2/6/91.

Other attempts to establish systems of absolute control, such as the Nazis and the Fascists, fell far short of their goal. Albert Speer's *INSIDE THE THIRD REICH*, conveys an impression of semi-coordinated anarchy. The CPSU, in contrast, not only nationalized the economy; they attempted to nationalize the minds of the people. They attempted, by mass repression and terror, to create the "new communist man," who would accept in perpetuity, the right of the Party to rule, and Marxism-Leninism as the alpha and omega of social, economic, and political wisdom.

"The existence of the communist dictatorship depends on the ability of the government to control the people's minds – and on the extent of that control. Stalin's brilliant idea was to put a good portion of the population on a sort of probation system, without their realizing it – one that would seem attractive and prestigious to its members. His success was astonishing. No prison is more stable or reliable than a self-service one. The prisoners there justify the restrictions on them and fully cooperate with the guards. In fact, they do not completely realize that they are prisoners."

Victor Orlov, "Inside Russia's Secret World.", The Washington Post, 11/20/88.

The NKVD /KGB were the cement that held the entire structure together. Were it not for them, the whole system would have collapsed like a house of cards, or been torn to shreds by its oppressed inmates. The Party elite repaid the NKVD/KGB by granting them extensive privileges, and almost unlimited power. They injected themselves into every form of association in the Soviet Union, not only to suppress or exterminate any actual or potential opposition, but, to actively assist in promoting the Party's ideology and programs.

"The vastness of the Soviet state's machinery for internal spying and repression is in itself an index to the extent and ubiquity of terror. Never before, not even in a world that included German Nazism and Italian fascism, has a regime spawned such gigantic organs of surveillance, denunciation, punishment, censorship, and intimidation. No government in modern time, except perhaps

Communist China, has invented so many 'crimes against the state' or applied the death penalty so extensively."
Lyons, op. cit., p. 356.

Terror was indispensable to the maintenance of Party supremacy, in fact, Lenin openly advocated its incorporation into the legal system:

"Court trials must not supercede the terror. To promise that they would do so would be self-deception or deceit; it (the terror) should be put on a definite basis and legalized as a matter of principle, clearly, without hypocrisy or embellishments."
Herbert McClosky and John E. Turner, *THE SOVIET DICTATORSHIP,* quoting Lenin, p. 444.

To lend proper perspective to any study of the Soviet secret police system, one must first examine its predecessor, the Tsarist secret police – the Okhrana. The Okhrana employed about 5000 full-time agents, plus several thousand part-time informers; the maximum number of political and criminal prisoners never exceeded 184,000 under the Tsars. Stalin's chief prosecutor, Andrei Vishinsky, estimated that in 1913, there were 32,000 political and criminal prisoners in the Tsar's prisons. In the five years between 1919 and 1924, it is estimated that the CHEKA executed at least 200,000 people, compared with 14,000 executed during the last fifty years of the Tsar's rule. Alan Bullock, *HITLER AND STALIN,* Alfred A. Knopf, NYC, 1992, p.61.

The CPSU's political police system was founded on 20 December 1917, as the CHEKA, under Felix Dzerzhinsky, who announced openly in June 1918 "we stand for organized terror." It went through periodic reorganizations and name changes: OGPU, NKVD, NKGB, MGB, MVD, and finally KGB.* It showed its true face early, when it, not the Nazis, established the world's first extermination camp in 1921, the Kolgomor Camp, near Arkangelsk. (Lyons, op. cit., p. 356.) It grew like a virus; by the mid-thirties it reached a strength of two million full-time agents, plus about 20 million part-time informers – "Stukachi". By 1939, out of a total labor force of 78,811,000, there were approximately 2,126,000 guards and watchmen, plus over 2,000,000 members of the NKVD.

Robert Conquest, *THE GREAT TERROR*, p.302.

* CHEKA (1917-22) Chrezychaynaya Komissiya Po Borbe S Kontrrevolutsiyey I Sabotazhem. All Russian Extraordinary Commission for Combating Counter-Revolution and Sabotage.

OGPU (1922-34) Obedinennoe Gosudarstvennoe Politicheskoe Upravlenie. United State Political Administration.

NKVD (1934-43) Norodnyi Kommissariat Vnutrennikh Del. Peoples Commissariat of Internal Affairs.

NKGB (1943-46) Norodnyi Kommissariat Gosudarstvennoi Bezopasnosti. Peoples Commissariat of State Security.

MGB (1946-53) Ministerstvo Gosudarstvennoi Bezopasnosti. Ministry of State Security.

MVD (1953) Ministerstvo Vnutrennikh Del. Ministry of Internal Security.

KGB (1953-91) Komitet Gosodarstvennoi Bezopasnosti. Committee for State Security.

The number of prisoners, primarily political, also grew exponentially. By the time of the German invasion in 1941, there were about thirteen million prisoners in the Gulag. After World War II, the number grew to somewhere between 20 million and 30 million, as all returning POWs, all Soviet citizens who had been forced to work in German factories, and any people in the German occupied zones, suspected of collaboration, were shipped to the Gulag.

The leaders of the political police always ranked near the top of the Party hierarchy. The "dreadful dwarf " Nikolai

Yezhov who Stalin placed in command of the NKVD during the Great Purge, was the first head of the political police to be made a member of the Secretariat of the Central Committee. "Little Niki" was chief of the NKVD between 1935 and 1938; a period that came to called "Yezhovshchina."

> "The K.G.B. is the real government in this country.... It is easy enough to be fooled by all the government bureaux, committees, agencies, and departments. They do all the running of the house. But behind them is always the K.G.B., the real power."
> An Observer, *MESSAGE FROM MOSCOW*, p. 65.

The following attempts to portray some elements of KGB structure. The NKVD in the 1930s and during World War II was organized and operated in much the same way. The command element of the KGB, the National Directorate, operated at the national, republic, and regional levels; with a strength of 600,000 to 1,000,000; it maintained control of all KGB, and Ministry of Defense military forces, as well as the Militia, the Fire Command, and miscellaneous organs. These National Directorate personnel controlled all branches of industry, agriculture, commerce, transport, education, and culture. They controlled all elements of the government and the Party, except for the very pinnacle of the Party elite, in whose behalf this vast instrument of control was wielded.

The precise numerical strength of the forces at the disposal of the KGB are not known. No reliable information about any component of the police structure was released by the government; in this sense the entire apparatus was "secret". However, I have compiled a table of the estimated strength of the KGB, from a number of sources, including:

Robert Conquest, *THE SOVIET POLICE SYSTEM,* p.26.
Ronald Hingley, *THE RUSSIAN SECRET POLICE,* p.269.

J. T. Reitz, "Soviet Defense-Associated Activities Outside the Minister of Defense, Economic Performance and the Military Burden in the Soviet Union,"1970. Joint Economic Committee of the Congress of the U. S.

KGB Directorate	800,000
Internal Troops	350,000
Border Troops	360,000
Guard Troops	175,000
Convoy Troops	125,000
Railway Troops	100,000
Militia	900,000
	2,810,000

Several elements of the National Directorate are worthy of special mention:

Directorate of Military Counterintelligence (Glavnoe upravlenie Kontrrazvedki – GUKR formerly SMERSH)

GUKR's principal mission was to watch the military for any signs of anti-Party activity. GUKR Special Sections (0sobyi otdel – 00) were the most powerful element in the military establishment; no officer was promoted without 00 approval.

Economic Directorate (Ekonomicheskoe upravlenie – EKU)

The EKU watched every element of industry, trade, and agriculture to guard against malpractice and sabotage; it supervised the Gulag enterprises, and oversaw the execution of GOSPLAN; the USSR's economic master plan; collating economic data from all branches of industry and agriculture. It would be comparable to placing responsibility for supervising a U. S. national economic plan for all commerce and industry in the hands of the CIA and FBI.

Foreign Intelligence Directorate (Inostrannoe upravlenie – INU)

The INU performed a variety of international intelligence, espionage, and subversion missions. The Mobile Section, formerly titled the Section for Terror and Diversion, was responsible for assassination, kidnapping, and sabotage abroad. The backup muscle of the KGB repression apparatus, was the Party's private elite military establishment. The Party, of course, had the regular military establishment at their disposal, but those forces had primarily an external strategic mission; whereas the KGB forces functioned almost entirely as an internal control instrument.

There were five major elements of the KGB military arm:

Internal Troops (Vnutrennie voiska MVD)

These troops had four main tasks:

Prevent coup d'etats against the Party;

Crush any mutinies within the military;

Crush anti-communist rebellion; guerilla warfare; or outside attempts to organize resistance groups;

Carry out mass repressions like collectivization, purges, or deportations to the Gulag.

They had a strength of between 250,000 and 500,000 men, and were strategically located near potential trouble spots throughout the country. They were an elite force, carefully selected for ideological reliability, and "represent the best disciplined, trained, equipped, armed and paid troops in the Soviet Union." They were organized into divisions of ten to twenty thousand men, brigades and battalions. They had infantry, armored, and artillery units. They also had their own air force. They were the first units to be given any new equipment; and usually had higher firepower and mobility than comparable units of the Red Army.

Many of these punitive units were composed of Mongols or other Oriental types, who did not speak or understand Russian, and who were therefore immune to persuasion by rebelling troops of the regular army. During World War II, such units called "blocking troops" were stationed behind the front lines to shoot any regular army or Gulag soldiers who attempted to retreat or desert. Such units were called in during the Hungarian Revolution to exterminate the regular army units who had gone over to the side of the Hungarian Rebels, or were refusing to fight them. To the eternal shame of the West, the only support the Hungarians received was from Soviet soldiers, for which they paid the supreme price. Mongol MVD units hunted them down like animals, and exterminated them to a man.

Guard Troops

These troops performed a wide range of guard duties, the most important being to guard Party leaders, slave labor camps, and government buildings. They also guarded the production, storage and distribution of nuclear equipment and warheads.

Convoy Troops

These troops were responsible for escorting arrested people, including slave laborers, being shipped to the Gulag, and nationalities being relocated. They also guarded the vast transportation system.

Border Troops (Proganichnye voiska KGB)

This command was similar to the Internal Troops, but had much more active day to day duties. They were responsible for guarding the land, sea, and air frontiers of the Soviet Union; not only to prevent penetration by foreign agents, but primarily to prevent Soviet citizens from escaping the Worker's Paradise. As with the punitive troops, these men were carefully screened for ideological reliability; orphans were ineligible, since they would have no one to serve as hostage to prevent their own escape.

The Militia (Militsiia MVD)

Most studies of the Soviet police system tend to dismiss the Militia as just another police force, performing the usual functions of these institutions. Aside from the fact they were a national police force; the Militia played a much more vital role in the overall surveillance process than is the case with police forces in most other parts of the world.

As previously noted, aside from 900,000 full-time Militiamen, there was a vast ancillary network, numbering in the tens of millions, who were obliged to assist them. These were the People's Squads; the Konsomol auxiliaries; the Brigades; the "Street Committees"; the "Rural Executives" (one for every 300 rural inhabitants); at least one "House Administrator" and night watchman for every apartment building, factory, school, etc. The house administrators and night watchmen checked the papers, and maintained a register of every person who entered or left; and stayed aware of the nature of all activity that took place in the building. All these ancillary personnel were legally responsible for reporting any form of suspicious activity to the Militia. This did not begin with Stalin. Starting in the seventeenth century, the law demanded the death penalty for failure to report a crime committed or intended. These people were not a part, except coincidently, of the NKVD/KGB's network of secret informers, whose number was estimated to be ten percent of the population.

The Militia performed all the usual police functions such as crime and traffic control, licensing, maintenance of order, etc.; they also administered the internal and international passport and travel control system. It was almost impossible for anyone in the Soviet Union to do anything about which some arm of the NKVD/KGB was not kept informed. To penetrate the family unit, the Party through its many youth organizations and the school system, taught and pressured children to inform on their parents. The fundamentally clandestine nature of the whole Communist system was demonstrated at an early date, when the regime made a national hero of Pavlik Morozov, a twelve year old boy, who in 1932 denounced his father as a grainhoarder. The authorities shot his parents; outraged neighbors killed Pavlik; the Party made the little rat a hero.

The Komsomol's Palace of Culture of the Red Pioneers in Moscow is named after him.

The NKVD/KGB had many other components designed to make the control system foolproof. They operated their own communication system, which was independent of government and military networks. They were also responsible for monitoring and jamming foreign broadcasts. As in *1984*, the KGB organized and operated underground groups, such as guerrilla bands, in order to entice and ensnare oppositionists. Reportedly, when foreign governments or outside anti-communist organizations landed agents inside the Soviet Union to form or support guerrilla groups, they found themselves enlisting KGB personnel, or joining KGB operated "guerrilla" bands.

For the United States to physically duplicate the KGB, it would have had to combine the CIA, FBI, NSA, the Secret Service, the Coast Guard, all the state and local police forces; and back them up with an elite military force, such as the Marine Corp. As we have seen, these organizations would have to be backed-up by perhaps 30 million covert part-time "stool pigeons", plus an equal number of overt finks and busy-bodies, such as block chairmen and neighborhood administrators.

Most authorities estimate that it cost the Soviet Union approximately 40% of its GNP to support the regular military establishment of approximately four million men. If we total up the military and paramilitary forces of the KGB, they rivaled the regular military establishment in size. But as we have seen, that was far from being the whole picture; the KGB had a vast horde of full-time and part-time informers that numbered perhaps 30 million people. It is reasonable to assume that this vast horde of the control apparatus must have cost almost as much as the regular military establishment, i.e., 20% to 30% of the GNP. This leads to the staggering possibility that the Soviet Union spent on the order of 60% to 70% of their GNP to support the military and the internal control apparatus. It is small wonder they were a third world economy.

"In this country there is only one master. Us. The KGB. We are known as the sword and shield of the Party, but in reality, we serve neither the Party nor the State, and certainly not the people. We serve ourselves. Even the military fear us and they have guns too. But we've discovered the ultimate weapon is illusion. We give the illusion that we are everywhere, so people dare not even whisper our name." The KGB "system ... finds merit in cruelty and uses terror as a management tool." Nelson Demille, *THE CHARM SCHOOL*.

During the Great Purge, Stalin perfected the machinery of absolute control by the Party apparatus. First, he used the NKVD to exterminate the old Party, government, and military command personnel; then he used the new Party apparatus and NKVD personnel to exterminate the old power structure of the NKVD. The mass exterminations and imprisonments, coupled with the trumped-up and phony "show trials", were designed to destroy the concept of truth, and to impose henceforth unquestioning acceptance of Stalin's absolute authority.

"The Christian ethic, with its concept of right and wrong has been shaken loose and driven out of the popular consciousness. It has been replaced by what the regime calls 'class morality' which really means: 'Good is what at any given moment is required by authority'". Andrei Amalrik, *WILL THE SOVIET UNION SURVIVE UNTIL 1984*, p. 37.

NKVD personnel, before the Purge period, were niggling, self-righteous functionaries, who were at best oafishly indifferent to the horrible suffering and death they were inflicting; many were deliberately brutal. However, these men were "humanitarian" compared to those the "bloodthirsty dwarf" Nicolai Yezhov brought in. Yezhov proceeded to systematically exterminate any NKVD personnel who were known to have shown any signs of compassion; thus the composition of the organization rapidly descended the scale from sadistical oafs to monsters. Yezhov's troopers were young "Clockwork Orange" thugs, without a shred of human feeling. Cruelty raged pandemic. In one small provincial town, the chief of police amused himself by sitting in his window beckoning to passers-by and arresting those who approached; they disappeared forever.

To compound the felony, during this era the attention of the Terror Machine was focused to a disproportionate extent on the educated, gifted, and intelligent, who constitute such a thin veneer of civilization in all countries. However, slaughter of the intelligentsia didn't begin with Stalin. Lenin hated the intelligentsia more than any other group; he made their extermination a priority of the Party. When Gorky tried to get Lenin to stop their slaughter, he wrote to him: "the intelligentsia is the brain of the nation." Lenin wrote back: "It is not the brain, it's the shit." On another occasion, Lenin sent a telegram demanding accelerated extermination of academia, saying: "We're not shooting enough professors."

Tatyana Tolstaya, "In Cannibalistic Times," The New York Times Review, 4/11/91, pp.3-6.

Lenin and Stalin believed that State-sponsored violence and terror were the most efficient way to achieve their mammoth objectives. After all, an old Russian proverb says: "If you beat a Russian enough he can do anything, even make a watch." It is distressing to imagine how many Dostoyevskis, Tolstoys, and Tchaikovskys must have been blotted-out, never to brighten our world. To truly understand the fragility of mankind's grip on civilization, one should not lose sight of the fact that men such as Hitler, Himmler, Lenin, and Stalin did not personally commit these atrocities. The victims were guarded, tortured, and exterminated by petty functionaries who were usually aware of the fact that most of their victims were innocent of any crime, but who hid behind the eternal slogan of their breed: "just doing my job". These are the types who have willingly carried-out the dirty work of all great tyrannies in history, usually with no more motivation than holding on to their despicable little jobs.

The villains were not to be found just among the police and bureaucrats; many of the victims of the Collectivization period owed their fate to envious, spiteful, or greedy neighbors, who denounced them as "kulaks" in order to loot their property, or just inflict suffering on someone they didn't like. Again, in the Great Purge period (and since), many victims lost their lives or freedom as a result of being denounced by associates who wanted their jobs, or neighbors who wanted their apartment.

It was not just the petty functionaries who were willing to do anything to hold on to their jobs; this entire massive apparatus of terror was designed to guarantee that a small group of men at the top – the Party elite – kept their jobs and privileges and power to control and intimidate their fellow citizens.

"The MVD have the strongest possible vested interest not only in maintaining the present regime, but in strengthening it. They are fully aware that they are the most hated representatives of Communism in Russia by all the people and the armed forces, and after seeing the fate of the Hungarian secret police in 1956, they know what would be in store for them if the will of the people was ever allowed to be freely expressed. They are certainly even more fanatical in their support of the regime than most of the Party members, not out of ideological conviction but for their own physical safety."

D. G. Stewart-Smith, *THE DEFEAT OF COMMUNISM*, p. 272.

A quotation from *MESSAGE FROM MOSCOW*, summarizes the hypothesis that the KGB represented a mirror image of their masters:

"Who do you think rises to power in the Party? Men who are hard enough, cynical enough and crude enough to best the competition. Only narrow-minded, chauvinistic, anti-enlightenment types – the worst of the Russian lower-middle class – can get to the top. Coarse and stupid men; third-rate minds of a degenerate ruling caste. And besides, they're afraid. They must bring the whole country down to their level in order to rule it. Even if some of the Party apparatchiks are a cut above that, remember, they've given control of law and order to the KGB. They're the people who actually run things in regional and district offices – who have operational control. And they are made in the classical gangster mould with the classical gangster mentality."

An Observer, *MESSAGE FROM MOSCOW*, pp.70-71.

By the time the Great Purge ended, between five and ten percent of the population had been arrested. Inasmuch as each arrested person was forced to name several "accomplices", the next wave of arrests would have imprisoned twenty percent or more of the population. Thus, the physical saturation point had been reached, and the underlying objective achieved, i.e., total subjugation of one of the largest countries in the world by a small band of ruthless men. A dress rehearsal to test-prove a system for world control.

"Terror is in the fact that, to defend itself, the regime commits not one or another act of violence but repeats all such acts perpetually, so that they pervade every phase of the nations life. Terror is as real in its threats as it is in its acts. The constant threat itself is terror. Terror creates two camps: the wielders of terror and the terrorized. To the first, terror is daring, toughness and defiance – the first chance, perhaps in many centuries, at self-assertion. To others, it is grief, humiliation, dread. Between these two camps there can be no understanding, only bitterness and hatred. On one side there is intoxication with power, insolence and ever-growing contempt for subordinates; in a word – domination. On the other side there is fear of punishment, resentment, silent envy, fawning on superiors; in a word – slavery. The two classes are thus established, divided by a bottomless social and psychological abyss; the class of the soviet commissars and their henchmen, and the class of soviet 'subjects'."

I. N. Steinberg, *IN THE WORKSHOP OF THE REVOLUTION*, p. 138.

By inflicting over 70 years of continuous and sometimes massive repression on Soviet society, the Party's basis of rule was firmly established; unquestioning obedience under threat of unlimited terror. The basic problem lies in the fact that the Communist movement got started all wrong. As George Kennan said: the Bolsheviks:

"... were all men who renounced, as a matter of ideological conviction, the view that there were any absolute standards of personal morality to which one owed obedience. Usefulness to the cause of social transformation, as defined by themselves, was the supreme determinant of right and wrong in all human conduct, including their own. With relation to people outside the Party itself, this was indeed the only criterion. Here, dishonesty, trickery, persecution, murder, torture were all in order, if considered to be useful and important, at the moment, to the cause."

Boris I. Nicolaevsky, *POWER AND THE SOVIET ELITE*, p.xxi, quoting George F. Kennan.

In a word, they were Nechaevists.

The vast hordes of the CPSU and the NKVD/KGB were people who made the fundamentals of Nechaevism/Leninism/ Stalinism the religion upon which their lives were built. They devoted their lives to revolution, subterfuge, and sabotage --- "the science of destruction."

Joseph Stalin was probably the most intelligent, cunning, and ruthless ruler in history. He outwitted and outmaneuvered powerful opponents like Trotsky, Hitler, Churchill, and Roosevelt, as though they were children. After over twenty years spent exterminating all intelligent potential leaders, when Stalin died in 1953, there was no one around capable of filling his boots. The brains of the operation were suddenly dead. Stalin's successors were not in his league in intellect or ruthlessness.

THE SLAUGHTERHOUSE

"Kolyma, Kolyma, Chudnaya planeta, Dvenadtsat mesyatsov zima, Ostalnoye leto."
Kolyma, Kolyma, Strange planet, Twelve months of winter, The rest is summer.
Russian saying

The Nazi Party was in power 13 years (1933-1945), during this period they exterminated approximately 6 million people. The Communist Party of the Soviet Union (CPSU) was in power for over 70 years, and exterminated between 60 million and 130 million people. While names like Himmler and Eichmann are well known; very few people have ever heard of Yagoda, Yezhov, and Beria.

The Nazi Party no longer exists; following World War II, most of its leaders were tried at Nurnberg by the victors, and either executed or imprisoned. At Nurnberg, the world was treated to one of the most monumental spectacles of sheer hypocrisy of all time, when the greatest mass-murderers in history – the Communists – sat in pious judgment over the runner-up mass-murderers of history – the Nazis.

Inasmuch as the world already has been thoroughly educated on the atrocities committed by the Nazi Party, and judge their movement on this basis; logic demands that the nature and scale of the atrocities committed by the Communist

Party be examined, so that their movement may be measured by the same scale.

In order to comprehend the magnitude of Communism's threat to civilization, the scale of its crimes against humanity must be measured; its techniques of repression studied. Let us begin by attempting to calculate the scale in terms of sheer numbers. It is said that people no longer react to enormous crimes, however, in order to understand the magnitude of the peril to civilization, we must first grasp how far the Communist rulers were willing to go to maintain themselves in power. As Lenin said: "Quantity has a quality of its own."

First we will summarize the death toll from all other causes than the slave labor penal system, the Gulag; such as: the Civil War, Liquidation of the Bourgeoisie (the "Red Terror"), the Collectivization, Purges, etc. With this part covered, we will focus our attention on an area that has been consistently underestimated – the tens of millions of innocent people who perished in the vast Gulag.

Since the word famine is usually associated with natural disaster, a brief explanation is required of the circumstances surrounding the famines in the Soviet Union. The first famine resulted from a combination of damage inflicted on agriculture by the Civil War; a drought; ruthless requisitions of food, seed and cattle by the Bolshevik government; combined with their first drive to force the farmers off their land and onto the State collective farms. It was mainly a man-made famine, but was not deliberately planned.

Before the Revolution, Peter Stolypin, the Tsar's prime minister, initiated a program to create a new "sober and strong" yeoman class among the peasantry. He succeeded so well that Lenin was worried the Bolsheviks would have to abandon their plan to industrialize agriculture. These more energetic and resourceful peasants were the "kulaks" that the Party "liquidated" in the Collectivization program.

Stalin believed crash Collectivization would provide the enormous grain exports needed to finance his massive industrialization and militarization programs. Farmers tried to resist by undersowing and by killing their livestock. The CPSU retaliated with mass deportations and executions, and deliberate starvation. Five million land-owning farmers (kulaks) were sent to Siberia. Stalin ordered the Cheka to seize almost the whole 1931 harvest, which was small to begin with due to a bad winter. Mass starvation raged, particularly in 1932-1933. Millions died. Parents often ate their children. In the middle of this disaster, Stalin ordered massive grain exports, to pay for foreign machinery for the First Five -Year Plan. This famine was a deliberate government action, designed to crush the independent farmer, and force him into the State collective farm system. It was the only deliberate man-made famine in history.

It is estimated that there were approximately 10 million deaths in the Civil War (1918-1920), since there were many groups involved, we will attribute 5 million to the Bolsheviks as their share. Adding 5 million for the "War Communism" famine (1921-1922), and 2 million for the "Red Terror", we arrive at an estimated total for this period (1917-1922) of 12 million deaths which can be reasonably assigned to the Communists.

For the period of Collectivization (1930-1935), Winston Churchill used a figure of 10 million; this is the number Stalin quoted directly to him at Yalta. However, recently released figures from the central archives in Moscow, put this number at 22 million. This is probably a more accurate number since between 1931 and 1933, Stalin waged another brutal war in the Ukraine designed not only to enforce collectivization, but more importantly, to destroy Ukrainian nationalism and tradition. Out of a farm population of approximately 20,000,000, approximately 10,000,000 Ukrainians were starved to death or murdered outright. The NKVD systematically destroyed the

Ukrainian intelligentsia; all writers, historians, composers; even the blind itinerant folk singers were shot.

> From all over the Ukraine, the Party assembled all the blind folk singers for the First All-Ukrainian Congress of Lirniki and Banduristy (folk singers) to discuss their future. Stalin had announced that: "Life is better, life is merrier." Hundreds of blind singers happily gathered at the Congress. The NKVD shot them all.
> Rummell, op. cit., p. 91.

Stalin's hatred of the Ukrainians dated back to their revolt against the Bolsheviks in 1920. This had led directly to the humiliating defeat of Stalin and General Tukhachevsky by the Polish Army later in the year. Stalin never forgave the Poles or the Ukrainians.

The NKVD and local CPSU officials completely cut off all food supplies to the Ukrainian farmers. When the farmers started eating dogs and cats; party officials killed all dogs and cats. When they tried eating wild birds; party officials killed the birds. The farmers were finally driven to eating their own or orphan children. The NKVD then starved, poisoned, or shot all homeless orphans who had managed to survive the mass famine. To put this massacre in perspective, consider that 10,000,000 Ukrainians were murdered in Stalin's 1931-1933 holocaust; 6,000,000 Jews were murdered in Hitler's 1941-1945 holocaust.

As previously noted, recent discoveries reveal that the Bolsheviks killed approximately "50 million ethnic Ukrainians within the borders of the Soviet Union" between 1917 and 1991.

There are myriad estimates of the death tolls resulting from the various purges. During the period of the Great Purge (1936-1938), the NKVD arrested between 5% and 10% of the total population of the Soviet Union; on the order of 9 million to 18 million people. Many casualty estimates for this period have included deaths in the Gulag, which are being counted separately. Therefore, in order to avoid counting the casualties twice, Robert Conquest's estimate of 3,000,000 for those executed outright was used.

Before we begin our study of the Gulag slaughter, certain historical facts need to be cited to lend proper perspective to the incredible numbers that will be encountered. As previously noted, under the Tsars, the maximum number of prisoners of all types never exceeded 184,000 at any given time. Even Andrei Vishinsky, the CPSU's chief prosecutor under Stalin, estimates that in 1913 there were only 32,000 prisoners of all types, political and criminal, in Imperial Russia. It is also worth noting that the number of prisoners in the Nazi camps never reached one million in peacetime. Sheer numbers aside, objective investigators agree that prison conditions under the Tsars were infinitely better than under the Communists. Comparing Tsarist and Communist terrorism is like comparing a pimple to a cancer.

Under the Tsars, political prisoners, classified as exiles, had an idyllic life compared to that under the Communists. They were not mixed with criminals, and enjoyed a vast array of special privileges. They were usually joined by their families; they were permitted correspondence with friends at home and abroad; for the scholarly, this was a time of intensive reading and writing. Lenin wrote *THE DEVELOPMENT OF CAPITALISM IN RUSSIA* while in exile. The sportsmen went in for hunting and fishing; Lenin, Trotsky, and Stalin were intrepid hunters.

"Nadezhda Krupskaya, Lenin's wife, recounting their routine in Siberia, might be talking about a middle-class winter vacation. One of her letters to a relative does have a tragic note: the maid has just walked out on her, Mrs. Lenin reports, and she has been obliged to do her own housework!"

Lyons, op. cit., p 95.

Under the Tsars, it was a time of banishment from one's home and career, to a life in harsh surroundings. Among the populace, political exiles were generally held in high esteem, being referred to as "unfortunates" or "passion-bearers." In contrast, the Communist regime has always referred to political prisoners as "wreckers," "enemies of the people," "mad-dogs," "excrement," "insects," "vipers." This demonization of one's opponents started early. In his battles with the Mensheviks, Lenin set forth his principles on how to fight a political adversary. They became the standard practice of the Soviet press and their Western "liberal" imitators.

"The wording is calculated to provoke in the reader hatred, disgust, contempt ...calculated not to convince but to destroy...not to correct the adversary's mistake, but to annihilate, to raze to the ground, his organization."
Lenin, *Sochineniya, Works*, Vol. XII, 1947.

"The suffering of the inmates of these camps can only be compared to that of the Nazi extermination camps, but whereas the Nazis gassed their victims relatively quickly, the Soviets work theirs to death over a long period."
Stewart-Smith, op. cit., p. 329.

One should not infer from this that the Party did not engage in mass extermination; the extermination methodologies of the Nazis and the Communists provide some interesting contrasts. The Nazis usually gassed their victims and cremated their bodies to hide the evidence from their own people and the outside world. The Communists usually shot their victims through the back of the head. Since most of these executions occurred in Siberia, where the frozen tundra made digging difficult; the bodies were stacked in huge mounds, which were covered over with dirt; the hills then froze solid like the tundra. Former prisoners report seeing vast stretches of these ominous mounds all over Siberia – God alone knows how many bodies are in them. In contrast to the Nazis, the rulers of the CPSU wanted their subjects to know about the exterminations; the threat of unrestrained terror was their principal means of retaining power.

Actually, the majority of persons who were given slave labor penal sentences, particularly the political cases, were never expected to return. The standard sentence from 1937 to 1959 was 25 years; after 1959, it became 10 to 15 years. Those who somehow survived to complete their original sentence, were usually not permitted to leave Siberia.

Numerous sources have estimated that in the Gulag, approximately 33% of the prisoners died during the first year in prison; 20% to 50% commonly died in transit to the camps; the annual death rate thereafter ranged from 10% to 100%, depending on the camp and the attitude of the regime at the moment.

There are a wide range of estimates of the Gulag population in 1941. Conquest estimated 6,000,000 to over 15,000,000. Swianiewicz estimated 3,000,000 to 13,000,000. Kosyk said 13,500,000 was an underestimate. An NKVD colonel in the inspectorate of camp guards estimated 12,000,000 to 14,000,000. Other NKVD officials and many ex-prisoners estimated the 1941 Gulag population at 12,000,000 to 20,000,000.

The Gulag was a dry guillotine in which millions of innocent people were sentenced to slow death by abuse, exposure, malnutrition, and overwork. Winter deportations to the Gulag were in unheated cattle cars, in trips that usually lasted several weeks, resulting in death rates as high as 50% just getting to the camps. Once at the camps, Solzhenitsyn estimated an annual death rate of 98%, calling such an estimate "commonplace and common knowledge." In the Far Eastern mining areas like Vorkuta and Kolyma, estimates of annual death rates ran from 30% to over 100%. In Kolyma, a region six times the size of France, goldmining could break a strong man's health for life in three weeks; the same was true for logging in the Kotlas region.

Some of the following data and descriptions should serve to corroborate and render these appalling death rates more comprehensible. For example, it was common practice with the massive influxes of prisoners during the Great Purge and following World War II, to simply make the prisoners dig vast pits in the ground; roof them over; and herd the prisoners in. This was in Siberia, where winter temperatures range from -15F to -50F for six months of the year. During the Purge period, Stalin accused the NKVD of "coddling" prisoners, so felt boots were replaced by canvas shoes.

Of those arrested during the period of the Great Purge, Robert Conquest, in *THE GREAT TERROR*, estimated that fewer than 10% survived. Bear in mind that between 5% and 10% of the population were arrested in this period; that is, between 9 million and 18 million out of a population of 180 million. This would mean that between 8,000,000 and 16,000,000 died.

Eugene Lyons, in *WORKERS PARADISE LOST*, estimated a mortality rate as high as 30% per year in the worst camps.

Lyons, op. cit., p. 358.

"...during the first year about one-third of prisoners die."
Antoni Ekert, *VANISHED WITHOUT A TRACE.*

"A careful study of this has produced a rate in camps, in 1933, of about 10 per cent per annum. In 1938 it had risen to about 20 per cent."
S. Swianiewicz, *FORCED LABOUR AND ECONOMIC DEVELOPMENT*, p.17.

In some camps, the death rate approached or exceeded 100% per year; in the Turkestan camps it reached 94%; generally speaking, anyone sentenced to 8 to 10 years was given little chance of surviving.

D. J. Dallin and B. I Nicolaevsky, *FORCED LABOUR IN THE SOVIET UNION*, pp. 278, 280.

Professor Swianiewicz estimated that of approximately 440,000 Poles sent to the Gulag between 1939 and 1942 "… not less than 40-50 percent must have died during an average incarceration of around two to two and a half years."

Swianiewicz, op. cit., pp. 41-42.

Following the Red Army's capture of Kursk in February 1943, 3000 "Kursk collaborationists," accused of cooperating with the Germans, were sent to the Gulag; only 60 were still alive in 1951.

Conquest, op. cit., p. 533.

The Baltic-White Sea Canal, also called the Belomor or Stalin Canal, was built entirely by political prisoners and kulaks; about 700,000 died on the job. This was the first large scale construction project assigned to the GPU.

During the first year (1932) of the Dalstroy Project to develop the Kolima gold fields, only one out of 50 to 100 prisoners sent to the interior from Magadan survived. During the first ten years of Dalstroy (1932-1941), slave laborers were arriving in the Kolima region at a rate of 400,000 to 500,000 a year.

Dallin, op. cit., pp. 125, 137.

Before the prisoners arrived at the camps, many had been subjected to weeks or months of brutal interrogation, followed by several more nightmarish weeks of travel in unheated cattle cars. The prisoners were so weakened by these ordeals and the shock of trying to adjust to the severe camp conditions, that over one-third of those arrested usually did not survive the first year.

Arrested in the middle of the night, the prisoners were taken to jail and caged in cells that were designed for only a fraction of their number; particularly during periods of accelerated repression. The cells were vermin infested, the floors covered with a mixture of excrement, vomit, and blood; there was no ventilation, they froze in winter and stifled in summer; the sanitary facility consisted of an enormous latrine bucket.

The interrogation process went on around the clock, for weeks or months, during which the prisoner was subjected to an unending routine of bullying, threats, blackmail, beatings, and torture. The process commonly involved beatings with fists, truncheons, brass knuckles, or anything handy. Women's nipples were torn off with pliers. The victim's fingers were slammed in doors; he was kicked or stomped; his head was repeatedly dumped in a bucket of excrement, vomit and urine; or the interrogators would just urinate in his face. The days and nights were constantly pierced with the victim's shrieks. During the period of the Great Purge, NKVD personnel were sent to formal brutalization courses.

Some prisoners were subjected to the "conveyer" system, wherein they were deprived of sleep for extended periods by relays of interrogators. Between interviews, the prisoners were often kept in one of the many "Slots". These were chimney-like shafts behind a heavy steel door; they measured from 18 to 24 inches in width and depth; and six to seven feet in height; the floors were covered in several inches of stinking muck, inasmuch as prisoners were not let out to relieve themselves.

Those selected for execution, were usually taken to a cellar or garage, where they were ordered to strip and kneel-down.

The NKVD man then dispatched them with a bullet in the base of the skull. The Soviet police system never had official executioners; so any member was always on call for this duty. The NKVD executioners usually wore their black leather jacket and a strapped on pistol; they were nearly always drunk on Vodka; so that the arrival of a shipment of Vodka almost always presaged a blood-bath.

In Leland Stowe's book, *CONQUEST BY TERROR*, a Hungarian described his journey to Siberia. These trips usually covered about 2000 miles, and took about two weeks, since a major portion of the trans-Siberian railroads were only single-tracked, and Gulag trains were frequently side-tracked for higher priority traffic. The conditions he described agree with the stories of nearly everyone else who survived the Gulag, so they must be regarded as typical:

"Again we were locked up in unheated, sealed cars. It was midwinter and frightfully cold. This time the journey was indescribable. The trains crawled and then stopped for long periods. But they never let us out. Some prisoners went mad from thirst. Whenever the train stopped shrieks and cries burst out on all sides: 'Water! Water! In God's name, water!' The guards pounded the sides of the cars with their rifle butts and threatened to shoot. Or they paid no attention." "When we reached Lvov ... at last we fell out of the doors. Few of us could stand. We were beaten and pulled to our feet. I saw the guards drag several corpses from the freight cars. We had been pressed so tightly together that men gasped their last breath, but many were kept erect by their neighbors, who did not realize they were dead. Their bodies froze in these cramped, erect positions. Many prisoners emerged like madmen, and some never recovered their senses. Others were so ill that they died during the next few days...."

"People were dying, day and night. The death rate was very high. But the Russians were sending an average of 2,000 prisoners each week. At the time they were all being sent to the infamous Gulag camps in the Komsomolskaya region (in Siberia). Some of the Lvov camp employees admitted that 20 per cent of the prisoners died en route ... 300 or 400 out of each 2,000 dispatched eastward from Lvov by train."

Such horrible experiences as these were often only the first leg of the journey. In his book, *THE LONG WALK*, Slavomir Rawicz describes the incredible nightmare he and his fellow prisoners experienced, following a similar train ride, in getting from the rail line at Irkutsk, northeast to an artic camp near Yakutsk.

Rawicz's excursion to hell began in mid-November 1940, when he left Moscow's infamous Lubyanka prison, for a cattle car ride similar to the one just described. The train trip from Moscow, 3000 miles east to Irkutsk on Lake Baikal, took one month. The prisoners clothing for this first leg of the journey consisted of cotton blouses and trousers, canvas shoes, no underwear or socks; the freight cars were unheated.

Upon arrival in Irkutsk in mid-December, the prisoners were marched to a barbed-wire enclosure in an open field, where they spent the next three days awaiting the arrival of fellow prisoners. The snow was waist deep, shelter consisted of mounds of snow and huddling together; the temperature in Irkutsk in December was usually around 40 degrees below zero; the prisoners were still wearing their cotton clothing.

At the end of the third day, the prisoners were issued their winter clothing, consisting of thigh-length, buttoned to the throat, kapok-padded jackets, the "fufaika", padded winter trousers, rubberized canvas boots, linen wrappings for socks; no hats, no gloves, and again no underwear.

After approximately 5000 prisoners and 1000 soldiers had been assembled, they were ready to begin their 1000 mile march from Irkutsk, northeast to Camp 303 on the Lena river, 200 to 300 miles southwest of Yakutsk; this portion of the journey lasted two months; from mid-December to mid-February.

For this leg of the journey, the prisoners and guards were sub-divided into 50 groups, each consisting of 100 prisoners, 20 guards, and one heavy-duty truck. Each section of prisoners were lined up in a column of twos behind the open trucks, and hand-cuffed by one wrist to a long heavy chain attached to the truck's towing hook; a machine gun was mounted on a platform behind the cab of each truck. The security procedure during the march, was for six guards, three on each flank of the column, to be on duty for two hours at a time; the other twelve would be "resting" in the open truck.

The prisoners were thus marched twelve hours a day, seven days a week, no matter how severe the weather (three blizzards occurred during the trip), for two months. The steady, unchanging diet, from the time they left Moscow, until they reached Camp 303, consisted of one pound of bread and two cups of hot tea per day. Conditions and terrain were so severe that the trucks had to be exchanged for teams of reindeer for the last portion of the trip. Temperatures (Fahrenheit) in this part of Siberia, at this time of year, range from a low of about - 53 degrees, to a high of about - 27. At such temperatures, steel splits and tires explode. In the Kolyma region, a temperature of minus 97.8F was recorded. During blizzards whole camps died, including the guards and dogs.

Physically, the camps were usually surrounded on the outside by log stockades, with guard towers containing machine guns and searchlights at frequent intervals. Within this structure, there were usually at least two concentric high barbed-wire fences, sometimes electrified. Often wild dogs were leashed to a wire running between the fences, from one guard tower to the next. Former prisoners, in describing the camps, tell of listening to the incessant zinging of the rings on the wires, night and day.

The gates were always topped with one of Communism's ubiquitous signboards, containing the camp number and some inspirational message. Emblazoned on a cliff face at Kolyma was: **GLORY TO STALIN, THE BEST FRIEND OF THE WORKERS AND PEASANTS** and **GLORY TO STALIN, THE GREATEST GENIUS OF MANKIND.** Martin Amis, *KOBA THE DREAD*, Hyperion, NYC, 2002, p.136.

Within the wire, the prisoner's barracks were usually arrayed around a central parade ground. The barracks were bleak, bare, one-story structures, with few windows and often no floor. Inside, they contained row upon row of tiered shelves, which served as beds, and several wood-burning stoves. Except for a few model camps, which were sometimes shown to, or reserved for, foreigners, the barracks were horribly crowded, filthy, and vermin infested, with no facilities beyond the NKVDs ubiquitous large slop buckets – they should have been on the NKVD shields.

The camps always contained some kind of punishment structure, the "Shizo", called the Isolater or Cooler. These were usually nothing more than a small, low-lying, one room log cabin. It was constructed by digging a one or two foot deep hole in the ground, and erecting log walls and a flat roof, five or six feet above ground level. The floor and walls, up to the logs, were earth, which was frozen solid in the winter. It was a completely bare room, with no heat or facilities, beyond – you guessed it – the slop bucket.

Life in the camps was geared to work and meeting quotas, with the State striving to extract the maximum output from the prisoners, in exchange for the minimum input of food and amenities. The prisoners worked ten to fourteen hours a day, in all kinds of weather, typically performing heavy labor in mining, forestry, and construction projects. In 1929, Stalin met Naftaly Frenkel. Frenkel had a theory that the Gulag could be more profitable if the slaves were worked to death quickly. Frenkel convinced Stalin that most useful productive capacity could be squeezed out of a prisoner in three months. Stalin bought Frenkel's theory and applied it with alacrity. A three month life span became the norm at Kolyma and Kotlas – also at Auschwitz. Amis, op. cit., pp. 71-72.

The prisoner was assigned a daily work quota or norm; his performance determined the amount of food he received. The maximum obtainable was usually about 2500 calories; the average prisoner usually managed to achieve some level between that and the 700 calories a day given to occupants of the Isolater. The food was usually black bread, thin cereal, and watery fish or cabbage soup, prepared with ingredients that would be thrown out as garbage in the civilized world. Solzhenitsyn described the bread as "sticky as clay." The prisoners were constantly driven, threatened and beaten. Eventually most of the prisoners were killed by a combination of overwork, undernourishment, physical abuse, lack of medical care, and destruction of the will to survive. A certain percentage of "politically harmful" prisoners were periodically shot as an example. With Stalin's death, many criminal, not political, prisoners were released. Soon the populations began to rise again; old practices were reestablished. Anatoly Marchenko's *MY TESTIMONY,* describes conditions of 1966 as being just like the old days.

In their book, *THE SOVIET DICTATORSHIP*, McClosky and Turner provide an excellent analysis of the functions, effectiveness, and significance of the Soviet slave labor system. First of all, it performed a vital role in the regime's reliance on terror to maintain control. It constituted a constant, creditable, and frightening reminder to all citizen of the Party's unwillingness to tolerate dissent.

It provided the CPSU with a massive pool of cheap labor, with which to accomplish extremely difficult and dangerous work in the Arctic zones of Siberia; where free workers could not be persuaded to go. The millions of slave laborers were the "working capital" of the Communist system.

Bernhard Roeder in *KATORGA* said: "The Stalinist system was thoroughly understood by the Russian People, and particularly by us in the camp, for the basic principle of Stalinism is the camp---."

Vladimir V. Tchernavin's book, *I SPEAK FOR THE SILENT*, contains an excellent description of the economic aspect of the slave labor system:

"...the camps have slave labor. This personnel is actually the invested capital of the GPU enterprises; it takes the place of expensive equipment and machinery. Machines require building, care and fuel of a certain quality and ... quantity. Not so with these prisoner-slaves. They need no care, they can exist in unheated barracks which they build themselves.

Their fuel ration...food ... can be regulated according to circumstances; ... they work equally well on rotten salted horse or camel meat. Finally the slave is a universal machine; today he digs a canal, tomorrow he fells trees.... The only requisite is an efficient organization for compelling him to work ... that is the specialty of the GPU.

But that is not all. This invested capital costs nothing to obtain, as the slaves did in capitalist countries where slavery existed; the supply is limitless....

And then there is the matter of wages, salaries, social insurance, union dues, and so on.... The GPU does not have to bother about these."

Someday, when the complete story of the Soviet slave labor system is finally told, the names of camps like Kolima, Vorkuta, and Karaganda, will rank in infamy with Belsen, Buchenwald, and Auschwitz. Finally, quoting McClosky and Turner:

"The Soviet camp system in many ways reflects Soviet society itself. Every penal system mirrors to some extent the society it serves, affording a measure of the society's operative values and sensibilities. The repression that characterizes Soviet life is nakedly evident in the camps."

Herbert McClosky and John E. Turner, *THE SOVIET DICTATORSHIP,* p. 499.

As stated earlier, previous attempts to calculate the death toll in the Gulag, that the author had seen, did not appear to be consistent with well documented estimates of prison populations in various periods, when combined with estimated annual death rates. Herein lies concealed the most appalling story of mass murder in history. Now that the reader has a better understanding of why such fantastic death rates were possible, let us resume the process of computing approximately how many people were exterminated.

First, a list of estimated Gulag camp populations by year or period, was generated; since there was a range of estimates for some periods, an average was computed. These are, by necessity, estimates; needless to say the CPSU did not publish such data; they were cross-checked from a number of sources. Much valuable information was obtained from the hundreds of thousands of POWs, who were released after the death of Stalin in 1953.

Based on the estimates from these various sources, the average Gulag population by year is listed in Table1. Combining these estimates with estimates of the Gulag population from 1971 to 1988 and interpolating for those years in which there is no data, the figures in Table 2 are obtained. The population figures are graphed in Figure 1. Note that the peak populations occurred roughly during the period from 1940 to 1960.

Some of the above estimates may be conservative, for example, a figure of 16 million was used for the 1945-1954 period. By 1954, few of those sent to the Gulag in 1945-1946 were still alive. During the post-World War II period, the Party sent to Siberia any Soviet soldier who had been a German POW; all Axis POWs (Germans, Italians, Hungarians, Japanese, etc.); any Soviet citizens who had worked in Germany as forced labor; plus millions of Soviet and East European citizens who they had any reason to believe may have been tainted by the German occupation. In 1948, the International Confederation of Free Trade Unions published a report on the Soviet slave labor system, which listed 250 major camp regions; each containing approximately 100,000 prisoners; yielding an estimated total population of 25,000,000. Some estimates of camp populations during this period ranged as high as forty million.

Kenneth Colegrave estimates the government established more than 800 slave labor camps during this period. Some of the camps were enormous; David J. Dallin estimates that there were approximately 500,000 prisoners in the arctic Vorkuta coal mining area alone. Every town or village in the Kolyma gold mining area was a slave labor camp. The Kolyma population grew from 150,000 in 1937, to between 300,000 and 400,000 in 1940. However, such figures are misleading, since there was a continuous need to replace dying prisoners. In the Vorkuta and Kolyma mining camps, and the Kotlas lumber camps very few prisoners survived for one year. About 200 miles north of Vorkuta, across the Kara Sea, lies the 600 mile long island of Novaya Zemlya. No prisoner is known to have ever returned from its arctic camps. (*KOLYMA*, Conquest, op. cit., p. 13)

Using the above table of estimated camp populations for each year, a probable death rate for each year from 1922 to 1970 was computed as follows:

For the period 1922 through 1954, a death rate of 33% the first year, and 15% for each successive year was used, with 25% surviving, and being released after seven years. Following the death of Stalin, prison conditions reportedly improved; so for the period 1953 to 1970, the above percentages were modified to show 20% dying the first year, 10% in each successive year, and 42.5% surviving and being released after seven years. Such death rates may be a worst-case scenario, or may be representative of only the worst camps; even so, they deserve to be considered.

Using the above population figures and death rates, a table of survivors from the previous seven years was computed for each year; the total survivors were subtracted from the total prison population each year, to yield the previously unknown probable number of arrests each year. The number of deaths each year was then derived by subtracting the total number of survivors for that year, from the total number of survivors from the previous year. The complete table from 1922 to 1988 is shown in Table 3. Figure 2 shows the values in Table 3 plotted graphically. Note that the total deaths in the camps during this period of time was 107,148,000. The shaded background on Table 3 from 1954 onward indicates the period of time when conditions in the camps improved and the estimated death rates dropped from 33% the first year to 20%, and the death rates for successive years dropped from 15% to 10%.

One seven year period, 1932-1939, is shown in Table 4 and graphed Figure 3. This period was selected because it includes the period of the Great Purge, which has been covered in many excellent books, so that the reader may check out some of the assumptions on his own. As the table indicates, when all the yearly death tolls are added up, we derive a total of 17,209,000 just for this one eight-year period.

Returning to pick up data from our earlier computations; we had calculated that the Party has been responsible for the extermination of at least 25,000,000 people by means other than the slave labor system. Now adding the calculated death toll of 107,148,000 from the Gulag, we arrive at a grand total of 132,148,000 people who were systematically exterminated since 1917.

Because of the scarcity of reliable data for either the death rates in the camps or the total population of the camps, a study of the effects of plus or minus 10% errors and plus or minus 20% errors in the estimated death rates on total deaths in the

camps was made. Results of this study are shown in Figure
4. The results show that if the estimated death rates used
here were actually 20% lower than the estimated values, that
the total of 107,148,000 deaths would have been *only* about
80,000,000; while if the death rates were 20% higher than
estimated, the total would have been nearly 140,000,000. In
round numbers, the total number of individuals killed, both
out of and in the Gulag most probably falls in the range from
105,000,000 to 165,000,000, with a mean value somewhere
around 130,000,000. Roman Krutsyk of Kiev Memorial be-
lieves the 130,000,000 estimate to be correct.

"The Second Five Year Plan had assessed the population of 1937 as 180,000,000, but the census came
in with a figure of almost 164,000,000, or a deficit of
nearly 16,700,000 between expected and actual."
Iosif G. Dyadkin, *Unnatural Deaths in the USSR*,
1928 - 1954. Translated by Tania Derugine, Transaction
Books, New Brunswick, NJ, 1983. Cited by Rummell,
op. cit., p. 123.

It is interesting to note a heretofore somewhat mysterious
deficit in Soviet population statistics vis-a-vis the United
States.

U. S. - USSR Populations (Millions)

	U. S.	USSR
1913	97.2	139.3
1926	117.4	147.0
1939	130.8	170.6 (190.7) *
1956	168.9 **	200.2
1959	177.8	208.8
1970	205.2	242.6

* Includes Ukraine, Byelorussia, Moldavia, Lithuania, Latvia,
   and Estonia.
** Includes Alaska and Hawaii.

Kenneth Colegrave, *DEMOCRACY VS COMMUNISM*, p. 236.

The average natural rate of population increase per 100 between 1913 and 1957 was: U. S. – 13.5 % and USSR – 15.9 %. In 1913, the population within the present boundaries of the USSR was 60% greater than that of the U. S.; in 1970, it was estimated to be only 20% greater. Based on the above average natural rates of increase, the 1970 populations should have been: U. S. – 207.6; USSR – 342.3. Thus, the U. S. population was almost exactly where it should have been, while the USSR had 100 million people missing!

In August 1992, Russian demographers "announced they had determined there were 63 million 'excess deaths' in the Soviet Union during Josef Stalin's reign – 1923-53."

Richard Rahn, Weapons of mass disinformation, T*he Washington Times*, 3/21/05, p. A15.

Recapping, we have Solzenitzen's estimate of 66 million up to 1959; Memorial's estimate of 84 million; and my estimate of 132 million. In his monumental work, *LETHAL POLITICS*, R. J. Rummel analyzed hundreds of published estimates of the number of people killed by the CPSU between 1917 and 1987; these estimates ranged from 28,326,000 to 126,891,000. Rummel's own estimate was 61,911,000. Take your choice; either of them constitute the most massive crime against humanity in the history of the world.

The "liberal" establishment will attempt to discredit this study by nitpicking details. In anticipation of such time-worn strategy, herewith, I will concede that my calculations could be off in either direction. Whether the Communist Terror Machine murdered 66 million, or 84 million, or 126 million or 130 million people, the immensity of their crime against humanity is undiminished. Lenin's tomb still occupies its place of honor in Red Square.

In his first interview after deportation, Solzhenitsyn lashed out at Western leftist/liberals saying: "For you, this all counts for little. For you, my entire book amounts to nothing. You will understand it all when they bellow at you too: 'You're under arrest' and you yourselves trudge off to our Archipelago."

Nazism is now almost universally adjudged to be evil on the basis of massive exterminations. It is now known that Communism committed exterminations on a scale at least ten times greater than those of the Nazis.

Richard Grenier, quoting Stanislav Govorukhin, author of the Russian film, *No Way To Live*, says:

"The Soviet state is a criminal state. It was founded by criminals, and their criminality pervades the furthest reaches of their society. Mr. Govorukhin sweeps by Josef Stalin as an almost too-obvious manifestation of Soviet viciousness to the system's master-designer, master-architect, master-criminal: Vladimir Ilyich Lenin." He asks: How can a system that, from the beginning, withdrew all legal and human rights from individual human beings, killing tens of millions of them in the process, be anything but criminal?"

Richard Grenier, "Not-so-soft and melodious music.", The Washington Times, 3/7/91.

"Thanks to ideology, the twentieth century was fated to experience evildoing on a scale calculated in the millions---." A. I. Solzhenitsyn

Ideology explained "how individual communists could beat, torture, and murder by the hundreds, and then sleep well at night. Grim tasks, to be sure, but after all, they were working for the greater good." R. J. Rummel, *LETHAL POLITICS.*

Starting with Lenin, the history of the Soviet Union was one of protracted and unrestricted application of state power to demolish and then rebuild all social institutions to create a Marxist utopia. Lenin couldn't have stated it more clearly:

"The scientific concept of dictatorship means nothing else but this: power without limit, resting directly upon force, restrained by no laws, absolutely unrestricted by rules."

Lenin and Stalin created a unique state, which through the exercise of absolute power and unrestrained terror, applied cold-blooded social-engineering on a massive scale to create an Orwellian utopia. The Black Death (1347-1351) killed 75 million people; Lenin, Stalin, and their fiendish familiars murdered over 100 million people in cold-blood. This was a monstrous system, run by monstrous people. It lasted 75 years and came dangerously close to winning. It was operated by cruel and ruthless people in the Communist Party and its police apparatus. They were aided and abetted by millions of ordinary people who, often eagerly, informed on and betrayed their fellow human beings. The cost was appalling – over 100 million people. Yet this monstrous system is still admired by a majority of America's "intellectual elite", particularly in the media, Hollywood, and the universities.

This was the nightmare Stalin came perilously close to inflicting upon Europe, and perhaps the world, in 1940 and 1941. Any one of Stalin's plans could have worked and he would have gained total control of Europe. America would have been the only remaining roadblock to world domination. America in the 1940s was under the control of socialist utopians – the "liberal" establishment; Stalin's own "poleznye idioty" – useful idiots. This gang, who "love every country but their own," would have been delighted to serve as Stalin's "vanguard" in America.

Many recent books have generated Gulag death toll estimates that are ridiculous. In Anne Applebaum's *Gulag*, a high percentage of those interviewed appear to have been people who had maneuvered themselves into some kind of "trusty" job. In the chapter titled The Trusties in *Gulag Archipelago*

Two, Solzhenitsyn said that 90% of the survivors of the Gulag were trustees. (p.251) These were people who through bribery, fraud, or finagling got some kind of soft job in the camp administration. In the Gulag such collaborators were called "pridurki","donosila", "stukach","sheptun",etc. – all variants of informer, stoolie, collaborator. And "naklepat" – to squeal. In the Nazi camps they were called "kapos." Solzhenitsyn said: "To get those positions impudence, slyness, bribery were required; to hold such jobs ruthlessness and a deaf ear to conscience were required (and, in most cases, to be a stool pigeon as well)." (p.261)

POSTSCRIPT

For those reluctant to believe America could have been sold out to Stalin in the 1940s, it is worthwhile to briefly recall the mindset of the intellectual establishment of that era. As Paul Hollander observed in *POLITICAL PILGRIMS*: "Throughout the 1920s many American intellectuals were disenchanted with their society – its business ethics, crassness, obsession with material values ...." With the beginning of the Depression in 1929 "the defects of the capitalist system ceased to be abstract ... when people lost their jobs, savings, and investments."

For America's intellectuals the Depression confirmed all their worst suspicions about our economic system; they fell in love with the Soviet system as a reaction against the economic chaos and inefficiency they saw around them. As Christopher Lasch observed: "Radical politics filled empty lives, provided a sense of meaning and purpose. The left served as a refuge from the terrors of inner life." Socialism became the opium of the intellectuals. In Depression America books on Stalin's Five-Year-Plan topped the best seller lists.

Once the intellectuals had made up their minds about the essential corruption of the Western system and the essential goodness of the Soviet system, details were no longer important. They came to detest everything about their own countries and to uncritically adore everything about the Soviet Union.

G. B. Shaw said of the British system: "The bourgeoisie is rotten. The army is rotten. The monarchies are rotten. Above all parliamentary institutions are rotten."

British economist G. D. H. Cole wrote: "Much better to be ruled by Stalin than by a pack of half-witted and half-hearted Social-Democrats."

American editor Lincoln Steffens wrote: "I am a patriot for Russia; the future is there; Russia will win out and it will save the world. That is my belief."

American writers Corliss and Margaret Lamont wrote: "The direction in the Soviet, from both material and cultural standpoints, seems steadily...upward, and the problems those of growth. Elsewhere in the world the direction seems downward and the problems those of decay."

As Todd Gitlin said of the '60s radicals: "They were so eager to see the future work; they were hungry to believe that somewhere out there, preferably on the dusky side of the globe where people looked exotic, some decency was under construction."

During the 1930s Western intellectuals made glorious religious pilgrimages to the "Worker's Paradise", where they unquestioningly believed the indoctrination of the Party's massive propaganda apparatus. Malcolm Muggeridge described them eloquently:

"Their delight in all they saw and were told, and the expression they gave to this delight, constitute unquestionably one of the wonders of our age. There were earnest advocates of the humane killing of cattle who looked up at the massive headquarters of the Ogpu with tears of gratitude in their eyes, earnest advocates of proportional representation who eagerly assented when the necessity of a Dictatorship of the Proletariat was explained to them, earnest clergymen who walked reverently through anti-God museums and reverently turned the pages of atheistic literature, earnest pacifists who watched delightedly tanks rattle across the Red Square and bombing planes darken the sky, earnest town-planning specialists who stood outside over-crowded ramshackle tenements and muttered: 'If only we had something like this in England!' The almost un-believable credulity of these mostly university-educated tourists astonished even Soviet officials used to handling foreign visitors...."

Malcolm Muggeridge, *SUN NEVER SETS*, p.79

ZACHTO ?

Zachto? Why? What for?

During the Great Terror that was the first question asked by the arrested; the one they kept repeating in disbelief. The larger question is why did something as monstrous as the Bolshevik regime happen. The quick and easy answer is that the CPSU's police state became a working model of Lord Acton's warning: "power corrupts, absolute power corrupts absolutely." Stalin and the secret police did seize absolute power. The totality of that power is still not grasped by outsiders. Solzhenitsyn said Communism survived "not because there has not been any struggle against it from the inside, not because people docilely surrendered to it, but because it is inhumanly strong, in a way as yet unimaginable in the West."

Zachto? Why in the late 18th century, were an incredibly gifted and noble group of men somehow assembled in America to create a government of freedom and opportunity unmatched in history? Why in the early 20th century, were an incredibly evil and destructive group of men somehow assembled in Russia to create a government unmatched in history for brutality, terror, and murder?

Historically, people seem to be driven by some deep yearning to rally behind strong leaders and submit to their will. This seems to be true whether they are good or evil. Washington, Jefferson, Madison, Monroe, Adams were strong good men. Lenin, Trotsky, Stalin, Zinoviev, Kamenev were strong evil men. Hitler and Stalin were very popular with the masses.

People seem innately driven by the dream of creating heaven on earth, the perfect society – Utopia. But how you go about trying to build it becomes all important. The Bolsheviks said the ultimate goal of "from each according to his ability; to each according to his needs" was so important that any means were justified to reach it. Their maxim was "the ends justify the means." As it turned out "the means defined the ends."

Professor Alan Kors recently noted: "No cause, ever, in the history of all mankind, has produced more cold-bloodied tyrants, more slaughtered innocents, and more orphans than socialism with power."

C. S. Lewis observed: "Of all tyrannies, a tyranny exercised for the good of its victims may be the most oppressive. It may be better to live under robber barons than under omnipotent moral busybodies. The robber barons cruelty may sometimes sleep, his cupidity may at some point be satiated; but those who torment us for our own good will torment us without end, for they do so with the approval of their own conscience."

Table 1. Estimated Gulag Camp Population, 1922-1970

Year(s)	Population
1922	57,000
1923	
1924	88,000
1925	145,000
1926	155,000
1927	198,000
1928	
1929	242,000
1930	600,000
1931-1932	2,000,000
1933-1935	5,000,000
1936	6,000,000
1937	9,000,000
1938-1941	13,000,000
1942-1944	14,000,000
1945-1954	16,000,000
1955	15,000,000
1956	13,000,000
1957	12,000,000
1958	10,000,000
1959	9,000,000
1960	7,000,000
1961	6,000,000
1962-1966	4,000,000
1967-1970	5,000,000

Table 2. Estimated Gulag Camp Population, 1922-1988

Year	Camp Pop, Thousands
1922	57
1923	60
1924	88
1925	148
1926	155
1927	198
1928	200
1929	242
1930	600
1931	2,000
1932	2,000
1933	5,000
1934	5,000
1935	5,000
1936	6,000
1937	9,000
1938	13,000
1939	13,000
1940	13,000
1941	13,000
1942	14,000
1943	14,000
1944	14,000
1945	16,000
1946	16,000
1947	16,000
1948	16,000
1949	16,000
1950	16,000
1951	16,000
1952	16,000
1953	16,000
1954	16,000

Table 2. Estimated Gulag Camp Population, 1922-1988 (con't)

Year	Camp Pop, Thousands
1955	15,000
1956	13,000
1957	12,000
1958	10,000
1959	9,000
1960	7,000
1961	6,000
1962	4,000
1963	4,000
1964	4,000
1965	4,000
1966	4,000
1967	5,000
1968	5,000
1969	5,000
1970	5,000
1971	5,000
1972	4,500
1973	4,500
1974	4,500
1975	4,500
1976	4,500
1977	4,500
1978	4,500
1979	4,500
1980	4,500
1981	4,000
1982	4,000
1983	4,000
1984	4,000
1985	4,000
1986	4,000
1987	4,000
1988	4,000

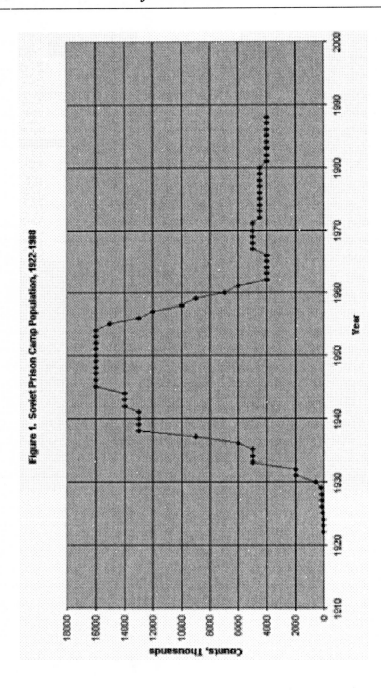

Figure 1. Soviet Prison Camp Population, 1922-1988

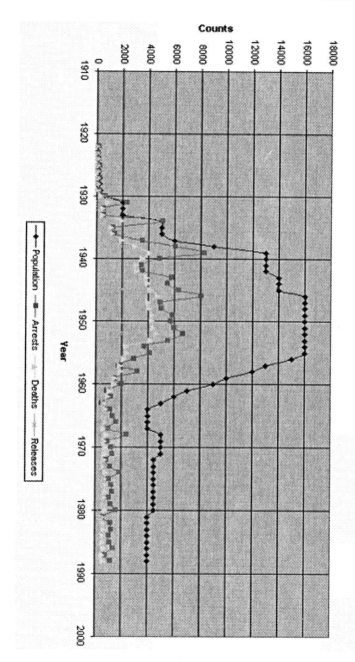

Figure 2. Soviet Prison Camps, 1922-1998

Table 3. Soviet Gulag Statistical Data, 1922-1988

Year	Camp Pop, Thousands	Arrests, Thousands	Deaths, Thousands	Releases, Thousands
1922	57	85	28	0
1923	60	17	14	0
1924	88	85	37	0
1925	148	114	54	0
1926	155	48	41	0
1927	198	104	61	0
1928	200	84	61	21
1929	242	119	73	4
1930	600	628	249	21
1931	2,000	2283	854	29
1932	2,000	473	461	12
1933	5,000	4994	1968	26
1934	5,000	1161	1140	21
1935	5,000	1174	1144	30
1936	6,000	2866	1708	158
1937	9,000	6715	3141	574
1938	13,000	8208	4089	119
1939	13,000	4813	3557	1256
1940	13,000	3367	3075	292
1941	13,000	3372	3077	295
1942	14,000	5511	3790	721
1943	14,000	5687	3999	1688
1944	14,000	6250	4186	2064
1945	16,000	7970	4760	1210
1946	16,000	4875	4028	847
1947	16,000	4876	4028	848
1948	16,000	5683	4297	1386
1949	16,000	5749	4319	1430
1950	16,000	5962	4390	1571
1951	16,000	6610	4606	2004
1952	16,000	5443	4217	1226
1953	16,000	5444	4218	1226
1954	16,000	3894	2381	1513
1955	15,000	2778	2158	1621

Table 3. (Continued) Soviet Gulag Statistical Data, 1922-1988

Year	Camp Pop, Thousands	Arrests, Thousands	Deaths, Thousands	Releases, Thousands
1956	13,000	1602	1822	1779
1957	12,000	2989	1900	2089
1958	10,000	1279	1458	1821
1959	9,000	2413	1485	1929
1960	7,000	697	1041	1655
1961	6,000	1104	923	1181
1962	5,000	354	673	681
1963	4,000	966	695	1271
1964	4,000	1182	638	544
1965	4,000	1785	759	1026
1966	4,000	873	577	296
1967	5,000	2339	870	469
1968	5,000	815	665	150
1969	5,000	1141	730	411
1970	5,000	1256	753	503
1971	5,000	1576	817	759
1972	4,500	466	595	371
1973	4,500	1808	814	995
1974	4,500	998	652	347
1975	4,500	1171	686	485
1976	4,500	1232	698	534
1977	4,500	1403	733	670
1978	4,500	813	615	198
1979	4,500	1526	757	769
1980	4,500	1096	671	424
1981	4,000	562	564	498
1982	4,000	1157	633	524
1983	4,000	1248	652	596
1984	4,000	934	589	346
1985	4,000	1313	665	649
1986	4,000	1085	619	466
1987	4,000	801	562	239
1988	4,000	1118	626	492
	Totals	158,548	107,148	47,380

Table 4. Soviet Gulag Statistical Data, 1932-1939

Year	Camp Pop, Thousands	Arrests, Thousands	Deaths, Thousands	Releases, Thousands
1932	2,000	473	461	12
1933	5,000	4994	1968	26
1934	5,000	1161	1140	21
1935	5,000	1174	1144	30
1936	6,000	2866	1708	158
1937	9,000	6715	3141	574
1938	13,000	8208	4089	119
1939	13,000	4813	3557	1256
Totals		30404	17209	2196

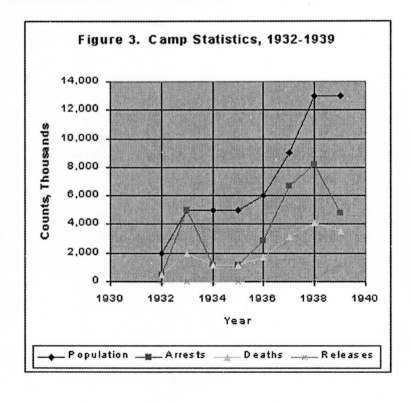

Figure 3. Camp Statistics, 1932-1939

Assumptions for calculations:

The values of death rates assumed in this book are:

For the Period 1922-1953

d11 = Death rate for 1st year of internment = 0.33

d12 = Death rates for 2nd and subsequent years of internment = 0.15

For the Period 1954-1988

d21 = Death rate for 1st year of internment = 0.2

d22 = Death rates for 2nd and subsequent years of internment = 0.1

To estimate the effects of possible errors in the determination of total deaths due to errors in estimating the death rates in the camps, the total deaths have been recalculated assuming +/-10% error in all death rates and +/-20% error. The results of these calculations are shown in the following table and are plotted in Fig. 4.

Percent Change	d11	d12	d21	d22	Total Deaths, 1922-1988, Thousands
-20	0.27	0.12	0.16	0.08	80,559
-10	0.29	0.14	0.18	0.09	93,387
0	0.33	0.15	0.20	0.10	107,148
10	0.37	0.17	0.22	0.11	121,990
20	0.40	0.18	0.24	0.12	138,097

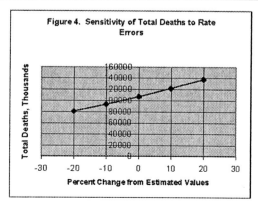

Figure 4. Sensitivity of Total Deaths to Rate Errors

Formulas used in calculations

$$\text{Arrests}(i) = [\text{Population}(i) - \text{Population}(i-1) + \text{Deaths}(i) + \text{Releases}(i)]/(1-\text{deathrate1})$$

$$\text{Deaths}(i) = D(i) + D(i-1) + D(i-2) + D(i-3) + D(i-4) + D(i-5) + D(i-6)$$

where

$D(i) = \text{deathrate1}*\text{Arrests}(i)$
    = those who died the in the first year after arrest
$D(i-1) = (1-\text{deathrate1})*\text{deathrate2}*\text{Arrests}(i-1)$
    = those in the current year who died during their
       second year of incarceration
$D(i-2) = (1-\text{deathrate1})*(1-\text{deathrate2})*\text{deathrate2}$
          $*\text{Arrests}(i-2)$
    = those in the current year who died in their third
       year of incarceration
$D(i-3) = (1-\text{deathrate1})*(1-\text{deathrate2})^2*\text{deathrate2}$
          $*\text{Arrests}(i-3)$
    = those in the current year who died in their
       fourth year of incarceration
$D(i-4) = (1-\text{deathrate1})*(1-\text{deathrate2})^3*\text{deathrate2}$
          $*\text{Arrests}(i-4)$
    = those in the current year who died in their fifth
       year of incarceration
$D(i-5) = (1-\text{deathrate1})*(1-\text{deathrate2})^4*\text{deathrate2}$
          $*\text{Arrests}(i-5)$
    = those in the current year who died in their sixth
       year of incarceration
$D(i-6) = (1-\text{deathrate1})*(1-\text{deathrate2})^5*\text{deathrate2}$
          $*\text{Arrests}(i-6)$
    = those in the current year who died in their
       seventh year of incarceration

Releases(i) = (1-deathrate1)*(1-deathrate2)^6
            *Arrests(i-6)
        = those in the current period who have been
          released after 7 years of incarceration

deathrate1 = 33% before 1954, 20% after 1954
deathrate2 = 15% before 1954, 10% after 1954

Population Check: (for the i-th year)
Population(i)–Population(i-1) = Arrests(i)–Deaths(i)
                                –Releases(i)

BIBLIOGRAPHY
HITLER: STALIN'S STOOGE

1. Bevin Alexander, *HOW HITLER COULD HAVE WON WORLD WAR II*, Crown Publishers, NYC, 2000.
2. Alan Bullock, *HITLER,* Harper & Brothers, NYC, 1952.
3. Peter Calvocoressi, Guy Wint, John Pritchard, *TOTAL WAR,* Pantheon Books, NYC.
4. Norman Carlisle, "the military inventor of the U. S. scorned," True Magazine, August, 1964.
5. Alan Clark, *BARBAROSSA* 1941-45, William Morrow & Co., NYC, 1965.
6. Conference between M. Stalin and Harry Hopkins 7/31/41, NARA, FDR Library, Foreign Relations of the United States 1941, Vol.1, General, The Soviet Union, pages 805-814, RLS 1/30/59.
7. Brian Crozier, *THE RISE AND FALL OF THE SOVIET EMPIRE*, Prima Publishing, Rocklin, CA, 1999.
8. James F. Dunnigan, Albert A. Nofi, *DIRTY LITTLE SECRETS OF WORLD WAR II*, William Morrow & Co., NYC.
9. Peter Elstob, *CONDOR LEGION*, Ballantine Books, Inc., NYC, 1973.
10. *FACTS ON COMMUNISM*, Volume II, THE SOVIET UNION FROM LENIN TO KHRUSHCHEV, Committee on Un-American Activities, House of Representatives, 86th Congress, 2nd Session, December 1960, U. S. Government Printing Office, Washington, 1961.
11. Bryan Fugate, Lev Dvoretsky, *THUNDER ON THE DNEPR*, Presidio Press, Novato, CA, 1997.
12. David M. Glantz, *BARBAROSSA*, Tempus Publishing Inc., Charleston, SC, 2001.
13. Heinz Guderian, *PANZER LEADER*, Ballantine Books, NYC, 1957.
14. E. J. Hofschmidt, W. H. Tantum IV, *TANK DATA* 2, W E Inc., Old Greenwich, CT, 1969.

15. Gwyneth Hughes & Simon Welfare with Robert Conquest, *RED EMPIRE*, St. Martin's Press, NYC, 1990.

16. John Keegan, et al. *BARBAROSSA*, Invasion of Russia 1941, Ballantine Books, NYC, 1970.

17. Amy Knight, *WHO KILLED KIROV*, Hill and Wang, NYC, 1999.

18. John Milson, *RUSSIAN TANKS 1900-1970,* Galahad Books, NYC, 1970.

19. Brian Moynahan with Yevgeny Yevtushenko, *THE RUSSIAN CENTURY*, Random House, NYC, 1994.

20. Douglas Orgill, et al. T-34 *RUSSIAN ARMOR*, Ballantine Books, NYC, 1971.

21. Janusz Piekalkiewicz, *TANK WAR 1939-1945*, Blandford Press, Poole, Dorset, UK.

22. Richard Pipes, *COMMUNISM*, The Modern Library, NYC, 2001.

23. Alfred Price, et al. *LUFTWAFFE*, Ballantine Books, NYC, 1969.

24. R. J. Rummel, *LETHAL POLITICS*, Soviet Genocide and Mass Murder since 1917, Transaction Publishers, New Brunswick and London, 1990.

25. Viktor Suvorov, *ICEBREAKER*, Hamish Hamilton, London, UK, 1990.

26. Ernst Topitsch, *STALIN'S WAR*, St. Martin's Press, NYC, 1987.

27. Albert L. Weeks, *STALIN'S OTHER WAR*, Rowman & Littlefield Publishing, Lanham, Maryland, 2002.

28. Barton Whaley, *OPERATIOM BARBAROSSA*, Phd Thesis, MIT, June 1969.

29. John Williams, et al. *FRANCE Summer 1940*, Ballantine Books, NYC, 1969.

30. Bertram G. Wolfe, *KHRUSHCHEV and STALIN'S GHOST,* Atlantic Press, London, 1957.

31. Earl F. Ziemke, Magna E. Bauer, *MOSCOW TO STALINGRAD: DECISION IN THE EAST*, Center of Military History, U. S. Army, Washington, DC, 1987.

BACKGROUND
1. Martin Sieff, "Soviet foxes eager to play Napoleon", The Washington Times, 1/10/91.

THE TERROR MACHINE
1. Andrei Amalrik, *WILL THE SOVIET UNION SURVIVE UNTIL 1984*, Penguin Books, NYC, 1980.
2. Abdurakhman Avtorkhanov, *THE COMMUNIST PARTY APPARATUS*, Henry Regnery Co., Chicago, Il, 1966.
3. Arnold Beichman, "Could this bear sell you the Brooklyn Bridge", The Washington Times, 2/6/91.
4. N. I. Bukharin, Izvestia, 3/30/34.
5. Robert Conquest, *THE GREAT TERROR*, Macmillan Co., NYC, 1968.
6. Robert Conquest, Gwyneth Hughes & Simon Welfare, *RED EMPIRE*, St. Martin's Press, NYC, 1990.
7. Robert Conquest, *THE SOVIET POLICE SYSTEM*, F. A. Praeger, NYC, 1968.
8. Nelson Demille, *THE CHARM SCHOOL,* G. K. Hall, Thorndike, ME, 1994.
9. Ronald Hingley, *THE RUSSIAN SECRET POLICE*, Simon and Schuster, NYC, 1970.
10. Roman Kolkowicz, *THE SOVIET MILITARY AND THE COMMUNIST PARTY*, Princeton University Press, Princeton, NJ, 1967.
11. V. I. Lenin, *WORKS*, XXV.
12. Eugene Lyons, *ASSIGNMENT IN UTOPIA,* Harcourt, Brace & Co., NYC, 1937.
13. Eugene Lyons, *WORKERS PARADISE LOST*, Funk & Wagnalls, NYC, 1967.
14. Herbert McClosky and John E. Turner, *THE SOVIET DICTATORSHIP*, McGraw-Hill, NYC, 1960.
15. Brian Moynahan & Yevgeny Yevtushenko, *THE RUSSIAN CENTURY*, Random House, NYC, 1994.

16. Boris I. Nicolaevsky and George F. Kennan, *POWER AND THE SOVIET ELITE*, Frederick A. Praeger, NYC, 1965.

17. An Observer, *MESSAGE FROM MOSCOW*, Alfred A. Knopf, NYC, 1969.

18. Victor Orlov, "Inside Russia's Secret World", The Washington Post, 11/20/88.

19. Robert Payne and Pearl Buck, *ZERO*, John Day Co., NYC, 1950.

20. Vladimir and Evdokia Petrov, *EMPIRE OF FEAR*, A. Deutsch, London, 1956.

21. Michael Prowdin, *THE UNMENTIONABLE NECHAEV*, Roy, NYC, 1961.

22. J. V. Stalin, *PROBLEMS OF LENINISM.*

23. J. V. Stalin, *WORKS XIII.*

24. Isaac N. Steinberg, *IN THE WORKSHOP OF THE REVOLUTION*, Rinehart, NYC, 1953.

25. D, G. Stewart-Smith, *THE DEFEAT OF COMMUNISM*, Ludgate Press, London, 1964.

27. J. T. Reitz, "Soviet Defense-Associated Activities Outside the Ministry of Defense, Economic Performance and the Military Burden in the Soviet Union", 1970. Joint Economic Committee of the Congress of the U.S.

28. Nicolas S. Timasheff, *THE GREAT RETREAT*, Dutton & Co., NYC, 1946.

29. Tatyana Tolstaya, "In Cannibalistic Times", The New York Times Review, 4/11/91, pp.3-6.

THE SLAUGHTERHOUSE

1. Martin Amis, *KOBA THE DREAD*, Hyperion, NYC, 2002.

2. Winston S. Churchill, *THE SECOND WORLD WAR*, Cassell, London, 1951.

3. Kenneth Colegrave, *DEMOCRACY VS COMMUNISM*, Van Nostrand, Princeton, NJ, 1961.

4. Committee of the Judiciary, U.S. Senate, The Human Cost of Soviet Communism, GPO, 1970.

5. Committee on Un-American Activities, House of Representatives, Facts on Communism, Vol.II.
6. Robert Conquest, *THE GREAT TERROR*, Macmillan Co., NYC, 1968.
7. D. J. Dallin and B. I. Nicolaevsky, *FORCED LABOUR IN THE SOVIET UNION*, Yale University Press, New Haven, CN, 1947.
8. Antoni Ekert, *VANISHED WITHOUT A TRACE*, Max Parrish, London, 1954.
9. Richard Grenier, "Not-so-soft and melodious music", The Washington Times, 3/7/91.
10. Eugene Lyons, *WORKERS PARADISE LOST*, Funk & Wagnalls, NYC, 1967.
11. Herbert McClosky and John E. Turner, *THE SOVIET DICTATORSHIP*, McGraw-Hill, NYC, 1960.
12. R. J. Rummel, *LETHAL POLITICS*, Transaction Publishers, London, 1990.
13. Michael Solomon, *MAGADAN*, Auerbach Publishing, NYC, 1971.
14. Aleksandr I. Solzhenitsyn, *THE GULAG ARCHIPELAGO 1918-1956,* Harper & Row, NYC, 1973.
15. D. G. Stewart-Smith, *THE DEFEAT OF COMMUNISM*, Ludgate Press, London, 1964.
16. Leland Stowe, *CONQUEST BY TERROR*, Random House, NYC, 1952.
17. Stanislaw Swianiewicz, *FORCED LABOUR AND ECONOMIC DEVELOPMENT*, Oxford University Press, London, NYC, 1965.
18. Vladimir V. Tchernavian, *I SPEAK FOR THE SILENT,* Hale, Cushman & Flint, Boston, NYC, 1935.

POSTSCRIPT

1. Paul Hollander, *POLITICAL PILGRIMS*, Transaction Publishers, New Brunswick and London, 1998

Printed in the United States
37659LVS00002B/307-330

9 781593 301446